THE REST OF YOUR LIFE
IS THE BEST OF YOUR LIFE

Finding the right path for the future is one of the greatest challenges you will ever face. LATE BLOOMERS is about confronting that challenge, and determining how you want to spend the rest of your life. It is about planting the seeds of growth and change.

LATE BLOOMERS is about making changes—reasoned and responsible ones—at the right moment in your life. It is about turning negative feelings into life-affirming action; it is about bottoming out and growing up.

LATE BLOOMERS is about not letting short-term gratification stand in the way of lifetime satisfaction. It is about satisfying your desires, achieving your goals, fulfilling your dreams. It is about making the rest of your life exactly what you want it to be.

LATE BLOOMERS

How To Achieve Your Potential At Any Age

Carol Colman

with Michael A. Perelman, Ph.D.

BALLANTINE BOOKS • NEW YORK

*To Ruth and Murray and
Bernice and Leonard*

CONTENTS

ACKNOWLEDGMENTS

This book has two names on its cover, but in truth, it is the work of many minds. First. I'd like to thank my husband, Michael Gerber, for his help and support in this and all my endeavors. I owe a special debt of gratitude to Michael A. Perelman, Ph.D., who served as consultant on this project, for his numerous observations and insights that are found throughout the book. I also want to thank my editors at Macmillan: Arlene Friedman for making the project possible, and Melinda Corey for her patience, encouragement, and superb editing. In addition, I'd like to thank my father, Murray Colman, for being such a tireless and thorough researcher, Jane Terker Perelman for her valuable advice, and Mary Trabulsy for patiently transcribing hours of tape. I also want to thank the many experts who gave so much of their time, including: Jeremy Robinson, Ph.D., Betsy Jaffe, Ph.D., Professor Larry Hirshhorn, Dr. Robert Butler, Marvin Cetron, Gunhild O. Hagestad, Ph.D., Arlene Kagle, Ph.D., Susan Schenkel, Ph.D., Martha Friedman, Ph.D., Adele Schiele, Ph.D., Loretta Walder, Ph.D., Judith White, M.S., C.S.W., Dr. Roy Walford, Carol Lane, Elaine Sorel, Dr. Paul Pearsall, John Crystal, Rabbi Richard Levy, Jerome Goldstein, Stuart Alan Rado, Douglas LaBier, M.D., and Dean Ray Brienza of New York University School of Medicine. I'd also like to thank my colleagues at WRFM Radio for their help and support. Last—but certainly not least—a very special thanks to the late bloomers who agreed to be interviewed and who so freely shared their thoughts, experiences, and insights.

INTRODUCTION

Are You a Late Bloomer?

 $\mathbf{M}$ any of us are so preoccupied with coping with our day-to-day responsibilities that we rarely take the time to consider what we really want out of life and how we can achieve it. And yet, during those rare moments when you stop and take stock of your life, you may have thoughts such as these:

- You know you want more out of life, but you don't know what it is you want.

- You feel unfulfilled, unhappy, underused. As one homemaker put it: "I didn't feel sharp any more. I felt like my brain was atrophying." Or as a pharmacist in his midforties described the sensation: "I felt wasted, as if I were suffering from an emotional cancer."

- You know *what* you want to do, but you can't figure out *how* to do it.

- You envy others. A friend tells you about an exciting new job, a career change, or a return to school, and you feel . . . miserable. You can only think to yourself, "Why didn't I do that?" (And what makes matters worse is that you know you could—and perhaps should—have.)

- You feel depressed because you know you have difficulty starting projects or completing them. You know you have the syrup, but you can't make it pour.

- You feel that you'll never find the dream or goal that truly interests you. And so you keep thinking to yourself: "What am I doing here?" or "Why am I doing this?" or "This isn't me."

- You think that other people are happier, more successful, and more (or less!) talented than you.

- You feel like your life is over because you've been fired, divorced, or widowed.

All of us have some of these feelings at one time or another. There is nothing wrong with having them. They signify that we are thoughtful, intelligent, and perhaps even ambitious people who, for good reasons, sometimes feel dissatisfied about the state of our lives. Where we may go wrong is in having these feelings and not dealing with them.

This book is about understanding those feelings, harnessing the energy you spend worrying about them, and making them work for you. This book is about people—late bloomers I call them—who have done just that and whose experiences can teach us a lot.

The term *late bloomer* is used by educators to describe youngsters who after years of doing poorly in elementary school suddenly—and unexpectedly—emerge as scholars. Others loosely apply *late bloomer* to persons like Grandma Moses who achieve enormous success very late in life. In this book the term *late bloomer* refers to people who after years of stagnating—feeling that they were not achieving all they could or were not doing what they really wanted— suddenly begin to fulfill their potential. As you meet these late bloomers, you will see that their lives are not very different from our own, and you will encounter some common themes.

Some of them, like us, wanted more out of life but did not know what it was they wanted. They searched for their life's path and they found it. For all of us, finding the right path is one of the greatest challenges we will ever face. *Late Bloomers* is about confronting that challenge and undertaking the quest to determine how we want to spend our lives.

Some of them, like us, knew what they wanted but couldn't figure out how to attain it. Then they recognized that if they stopped relegating their fate to chance they could have a direct impact on their destinies. So can we. *Late Bloomers* is about becoming the stewards of our own destinies, choosing and planning the seeds of our own growth and change.

Some of them, like us, knew what they wanted to do but

couldn't figure out how to do it. They were caught in an emotional tug-of-war between a felt need to take risks and a desire for security. Finally, as a result of their stunted development, their sense of comfort was surpassed by feelings of anger and frustration. They bloomed then, and so can we. *Late Bloomers* is about making changes, reasoned and responsible ones, at the right moment of our lives.

Some of them, like us, were torn between personal dreams of self-fulfillment and conflicting dreams involving the emotional and financial well-being of their families. Then, one day, something happened that made them see that it was time to reactivate some of their lost dreams.

Some of them, like us, felt it was too late for them. Then they realized that if their dreams were strong enough, with courage and determination they could make them come true at any age.

Some of them, like us, were gripped by envy, frustration, grief, or depression. They experienced a serious illness, or the loss of a loved one, or a painful divorce that prompted them to reexamine and turn their lives around. For them misery became a catalyst that triggered the blooming process. It can become one for us. *Late Bloomers* is about turning negative feelings into life-affirming action; it is about bottoming out and growing up.

Some of them, like us, had difficulty taking that first step. Others were great starters but never could make it to the finish line. Then they realized—for the first time really realized—what they had heard before: Success doesn't happen overnight. Along with this realization came the recognition that the *process of achieving* the right goal can be as satisfying and fulfilling as the achievement itself. *Late*

Bloomers is about not letting short-term gratification stand in the way of lifetime satisfaction.

Late Bloomers is about achieving our personal dreams and goals. In *Late Bloomers* we follow the three phases of the blooming process:

- *The Realization*—Recognizing that we want more out of life and are willing to make the commitment to achieve it.

- *The Quest*—Searching to determine what that "something more" is. We may resurrect old dreams or develop new ones.

- *The Fulfillment*—Identifying and overcoming the hurdles that have prevented us from attaining our goals.

We don't go from seed to flower overnight. It can take years—sometimes even decades—to develop, grow, and achieve our goals. For some of us it is a cyclical process in which we blossom, fulfill our dreams, and then, as our needs and desires change, we begin the process all over again.

The blooming process is no bed of roses. It is filled with many psychological problems and pitfalls. But we can overcome them. *Late Bloomers* is a guide to the blooming process and is based on the stories of men and women like yourself. These are profiles of real people—not composites—who, in most cases, are identified by their real names. (There were a few who for professional or personal reasons preferred to remain anonymous. In these cases I used a pseudonym, marked with an asterisk, and changed some of the details of their stories to protect their privacy.) I tell their stories in great detail for several reasons: first, to identify the events and influences in their lives that brought them to bloom; second, so that we can learn from their mistakes as well as their successes; and finally, because they are an unusual group of people whose stories are both fascinating and inspirational.

Late Bloomers is based on more than forty in-depth interviews with a diverse group of men and women ranging in age from thirty-two to seventy-two. I found these people everywhere. I was referred to many of them by professional organizations, graduate schools, friends, and colleagues. A few had been mentioned in newspaper or magazine articles in connection with their extraordinary accomplishments. What they all have in common is that they achieved significant things "off time"; that is, they did not follow standard timetables. A late bloomer is a thirty-two-year-old man who is the oldest student in his medical-school class. A late bloomer is a fifty-four-year-old woman who publishes her first book. A late bloomer is a thirty-six-year-old homemaker who lands a plum job on television. A late bloomer is a sixty-seven-year-old grandmother who joins the Peace Corps. And you, too, can join the ranks of these late bloomers when you start identifying and fulfilling your personal dreams.

Late Bloomers is the first book ever to examine the blooming process in such depth and detail. Although it may be the first word on this long-neglected subject, it is hardly the last. This book is only a preliminary investigation that I hope will focus some attention on this phenomenon. Much more research needs to be done before we fully understand why people grow and develop at different speeds and why some people bloom and others remain nipped in the bud.

Michael A. Perelman, Ph.D., a psychotherapist in private practice in New York who is also a clinical assistant professor of psychiatry at New York Hospital/Cornell Medical Center, worked as an adviser and consultant on this study since its inception. Many of the observations and insights found within this book are his.

Late Bloomers is filled with stories of people who did what we all want to do—and what I believe we all can do. They discovered (or rediscovered) what it was they wanted out of life and achieved it. The stories of these men and women will help us see that if we're willing to make the commitment, we *can* become the people we want to be.

—Carol Colman
September 1985

CHAPTER 1

Late Bloomers: Why So Many of Us?

When I told people that I was writing a book about late bloomers, I was astonished by how many of them quickly said, "You're writing a book about *me!*" Many of them were as young as their midtwenties. Their reaction made me wonder why so many of us think of ourselves as late bloomers . . . or hope that we are.

When we pause and take stock of our lives, many of us experience the vague, nagging sensation that somehow we are lagging behind. We feel that in at least some important respects we are not keeping up with the "others." Those of us who march to the ticking of a different clock often feel like there is something wrong with us. We look enviously at other people who seem to do everything "on time." These are the ones who graduate from school at the "right" age, marry in their early twenties, immediately pursue careers, and then begin families. But as you will see in the pages that follow, there are more of us than we think. Indeed, it appears that we are becoming a society of late bloomers—or perennials—who grow, develop, blossom, and begin the cycle anew at our own pace.

There are several explanations for this bumper crop of late bloomers.

One explanation is our extended life span.

At the turn of the century, the average life expectancy of a U.S. citizen was forty-seven. Today that is barely middle age. Current projections tell us to look forward to living well into our seventies and beyond. For those of us who stray from traditional timetables, this is very good news. The longer we have to live, the less it matters whether we do things "on time" or on our own time. We are liberated from the pressure of having to make important decisions "prematurely," such as selecting a career or a spouse, at a young age. And if we make a mistake after we do decide, we have more time to make midcourse adjustments.

The longer we live, the less likely we are to stay in one occupation or one life-style. The career that we found exciting and challenging at age twenty-five may strike us as tedious or meaningless a decade later. And sometimes changes will be forced on us. The advance of technology could render today's "hot" career bone cold tomorrow.

Late Bloomers: Why So Many of Us?

According to the U.S. Department of Labor, each year 9 percent of American workers switch careers.

We not only have more time to make choices, but we have many more options from which to choose. The social and economic upheavals of the 1960s and 1970s—the women's movement, the sexual revolution, the growth of technology—dramatically changed the lives of most Americans. As recently as the 1950s, for the vast majority of us life was an orderly progression of anticipated events. We completed our education at roughly the same time, married by age twenty-two, and stayed married whether we were happy or not. It was an era when sociologists wrote alarming treatises about the dangers of conformity and folksingers sang ironic ditties about "little boxes, little boxes, little boxes on a hillside, little boxes, little boxes, and they all look just the same." And those of us who were not "just the same" felt like outcasts. One man I interviewed told me that in 1960, when his thirty-six-year-old wife accidentally became pregnant, he was extremely embarrassed about the whole thing. "We had two teenage daughters who would be off to college in a few years, and so we were already planning on selling the house and moving to an apartment in the city. I was miserable at the prospect of having another baby, not just because it would put a damper on our plans but because I felt certain that everyone would know that it was a mistake. I mean, no one our age was having babies."

Today he and his wife would feel right at home strolling down Main Street with their baby carriage alongside the other parents in their mid- to late-thirties, who are having children at a faster rate than any other age group. While the majority of women still marry and have children in their twenties, there is little if any stigma attached to being an older parent. In fact, we are becoming more tolerant of a wide diversity of life-styles that have emerged within the past decade. The traditional family of the 1950s—a bread-winner, a breadmaker and their 2.6 Mouseketeers—is now in the minority. As the best-seller *Megatrends* notes, the traditional family has been replaced by thirteen separate household types, including such categories as "female head, widowed with children" and "male head, previously married, with children." The skyrocketing divorce rate (now 40 percent) is partially responsible for the emergence of these new forms of family life.

What this means is that our life paths will be filled with twists, turns, and forks that will offer the opportunity to make choices about how we want to live. We will experience what some psychologists call a "fluid" life cycle, exercising life-style options and moving from role to role. Freed from the burden of conforming to one life-style, we can shape and design our own life pattern. The time and order in which we do things will become less and less important.

Old assumptions about what we are supposed to do at certain ages no longer apply. A fifty-three-year-old man, for instance, could be a new father or a grandfather, and no one would be particularly surprised. A thirty-eight-year-old woman could be a pregnant executive just starting a family, or she could be a mother returning to the work force. A sixty-five-year-old could be living the life of ease in a retirement village or embarking on a new career. In short, we're doing things when we want to do them, not because we're expected to do them.

This doesn't mean that discrimination based on age or sex no longer exists. Unfortunately, it does. It's often more difficult for older people to switch careers or change jobs because many employers still prefer to hire the young. Some discrimination, however, is self-imposed. We start believing the negative stereotypes about aging, and like a prophesy fulfilled, we are defeated before we even begin. But if we fight these attitudes, we can win. In her late thirties, late bloomer Millie Brown, angered by the prevailing belief that life was downhill after forty, set out to prove that age need not prevent us from fulfilling our dreams.

Born and raised in Dubuque, Iowa, Millie was brought up in a comfortable, middle-class home to be a wife and mother. Married at eighteen, she had three children by the time she was twenty-two. By her late twenties, she was a divorced, single mother struggling to make it on her own. A series of odd jobs put food on the table and clothes on her children's backs. Millie, a trim brunette with shoulder-length hair, recalled that when she was in her twenties her view of life was very limited. "My goal—if you could call it that—was to work for some wealthy person cleaning her house. I didn't have any goals. I was so busy raising my kids, meeting the day-to-day costs, I didn't have any real plans."

After having remarried in her early thirties, Millie and her children moved to Connecticut with her new husband. Within two years her marriage broke up. "There had been a complete breakdown in trust," Millie explained. "He lied to me about several important things, and I no longer wanted to live with him."

The second divorce forced Millie to do some hard thinking about her life. "Up until that point, I was still looking for a father for my kids and a husband to support me," she said thoughtfully. "I finally realized that I couldn't keep looking for a man to take care of me. I was already approaching middle age, and I had to be able to take care of myself."

But Millie still had no idea how she was going to do it and—more importantly—*what* she wanted to do. To support her family, she took a job as an ice-skating instructor at a local rink. Although Millie enjoyed working with children, she didn't find the job challenging enough to make it her life's work.

As she approached her late thirties, Millie experienced one of the most difficult periods of her life. Back home in Dubuque, her mother was dying. Her three teenagers were growing up and nearing college age. How would she be able to pay their college tuition when she was barely managing the monthly bills? When Millie stopped worrying about everyone else, she would worry about herself. Here she was, approaching middle age, without any idea of how she was going to spend the rest of her life. Her job was a dead end, but she didn't know what else she could do.

Anxious and depressed, Millie would wake up in the middle of the night, tossing and turning and thinking until morning. One day, before dawn, too tense to stay in bed, Millie decided to go out for a walk. As soon as she hit the fresh air, she felt invigorated and even happy. She began walking briskly, and before she knew it she found herself jogging around the block, thoroughly enjoying the autumn scenery. From that point on, instead of dreading her sleepless nights, she would go to bed looking forward to her early morning run.

Although her problems didn't vanish, Millie found that she felt better prepared to cope with them, doing her best thinking before the day began. As she reassessed her life, she reached a conclusion that startled her. For nearly two decades she had either been a wife trying to hold together a failing marriage or a single mother struggling to maintain a family on her own. There had been little, if any, time for Millie to think about her desires or needs.

Millie asked herself, "What do I really want?" For the first time in her life, Millie was forced to think about herself— her likes, dislikes, values and beliefs. On one subject she had very strong feelings. As a woman nearing middle age, she deeply resented the negative stereotypes of people— especially women—over forty. On her morning runs, she would see joggers in their fifties and sixties who appeared more vigorous than many younger people. Millie had now found her mission in life: to prove that society's devaluation of middle-aged and older people was wrong.

"Many people in their forties and fifties seem to lose all the good feelings they had about themselves when they were younger. I was determined to show them that it doesn't have to be that way," she asserted.

Her yearning for self-fulfillment, combined with her need to prove that life was not a downward spiral after forty, gave rise to a new dream. Millie—who had never run more than a few blocks at a time—vowed that by her fortieth birthday she would compete in the New York City Marathon.

Millie put herself on a rigorous training schedule, running a little bit farther each morning. For camaraderie and support, she joined a local runners' club. After two years, at age forty, Millie achieved her goal by completing the 26.2-mile New York Marathon.

For Millie it was a turning point in her life. "It was very exciting," she said. "It proved to me that nothing is impossible." That same year, as a birthday present to herself, Millie enrolled in a local college to study writing. "It was something that I always wanted to do, and I no longer thought in terms of being too old to try something new," she explained.

Exhilarated by her success in athletics and at school, Millie searched for a new goal. It came to her on a boating trip with some friends, when she realized that she was afraid to put her face in water. Determined not to give in to her fears, Millie had a new mission. From other runners she had heard about the Ironman Triathlon in Hawaii. It was rumored to be one of the most grueling competitions in the world—and justifiably so. Participants were required to take a two-and-a-half-mile swim in the ocean, followed by a 112-mile bike ride and a twenty-six-mile run to the finish line, all within a seventeen-hour deadline. As Millie saw it, competing in the Ironman would serve many purposes. First, it would force her to overcome her fear of water. And, even more importantly, it would prove to the world that middle-aged women were capable of participating in high-endurance sports.

As Millie trained for the Ironman, she found the psychological barriers more difficult to overcome than the physical ones. "It's especially hard for women my age because we were taught not to do anything that would make us sweat. That was ingrained in us," she explained. "One of the hardest things was to convince myself that I was capable of changing a bicycle tire, that I could figure out how bicycle gears worked. Subconsciously I was telling myself that women aren't supposed to do things like that."

In the summer of 1980, Millie proved that women were supposed "to do things like that" when she competed in a smaller, less rigorous triathlon in Connecticut. The race consisted of a one-mile swim, a twenty-seven-mile bicycle ride, and a ten-mile run. Millie will never forget her joy when she crossed the finish line. "It was a thrill," she said. "Every time you stretch yourself, you run a little farther, or do something you didn't think you could do before, you feel better about yourself."

By her forty-third birthday, Millie had her day in the sun—and the wind and the water. In the fall of 1982, she completed the Ironman in Hawaii. There were times during the strenuous competition when she would have gladly traded all her worldly possessions for a few moments of sleep. But despite her fatigue, Millie kept going. As a symbol of the over-forty athlete, she was determined to finish the race. "When I was training, women back home would say to me, 'I'm proud of you.' Men told me that I gave them confidence because if I can do it, they can do it. I just couldn't let any of these people down," she said.

The "unsinkable Millie Brown," as her friends call her, has a new mission. To encourage more people to get involved in sports, she is writing a book on nonstress exercise. She also has a new career. Since 1983 Millie has worked as a consultant for Norelco's health-care division. And Millie hopes one day to write about her experiences as a middle-aged athlete. You can bet that if she ever gets around to writing her life story, it will reflect her motto: Nothing is impossible. "Don't be afraid to dream," she said. "Just go after your goals slowly. I started by running one block at a time. Start small and work your way up. Eventually you'll get there."

Millie succeeded in proving that arbitrary age barriers should not prevent us from fulfilling our goals. From Millie's story we can see that if we believe in ourselves and are willing to work toward our dreams, we will achieve them.

CHAPTER 2

Whose Life Is It Anyway?

"*I want more,*" Mark Rossi* said.

"I want more."

"I want more."

"I want more."

When I interviewed Mark, a thirty-two-year-old New York photographer, I lost count of the number of times he said, "I want *more!*"

"No matter how much I have, I always want *more!*" he shouted, attempting to describe the sensation.

Mark is not talking about material desires; rather, he is trying to describe a deeper, more basic, and more profound need for self-fulfillment. The desire for "more" is a feeling most of us have experienced. Coming to grips with this desire by recognizing that we not only want more but are able to achieve more is the first and most critical step in the blooming process. Many of us are frustrated and unhappy with our jobs, our relationships, or both. Yet we often ignore these feelings of discontent because to acknowledge them is to admit that we are ambitious to ourselves and, more, that we may have to make some changes in our lives.

The prospect of change is frightening. We may not be excited, stimulated, or fulfilled by the familiar, but we certainly are comfortable with it. As if the unknown were not scary enough, the prospect of trying something new and falling flat on our faces can be so terrifying as to be paralyzing. That is why before many of us can even admit— let alone come to grips with—the idea that we want more out of life, we must reach the point at which our need for change surpasses our need for security. Some of us reach that point when we "bottom out"—when we become so dissatisfied with our lives that we are finally willing to take some risks because we can no longer bear the awful pain of stagnation.

For some of us, an unexpected event—a divorce, the loss of a job, a life-threatening illness, or the death of a loved one—is the catalyst that provokes us into taking stock of our lives. When the rug suddenly is pulled out from under us, we are forced to confront many of the emotionally charged issues that we may have avoided in the past. We who felt we were wasting our lives decide in favor of doing something about it. In short, we say to ourselves, "I want more."

But knowing that we want more out of life is only the first stage in the blooming process. The next step is to figure out precisely what it is we want. In other words, we have to ask ourselves, "I want more of what?" Or, more precisely, "What is more?"

Of course, we all know that asking these questions is the easy part. Answering them is what's hard. Some of us have been propelled by necessity and circumstance and convention for so long that we feel completely lost and out of touch; we may wonder whether we will ever find our way back to ourselves again. Some of us are caught in the intersection of so many conflicting and equally compelling interests and desires that we feel incapable of deciding which way to turn. Some of us have yet to find an occupation that doesn't bore us within six months, and our lives are a collection of false starts.

You will see, through the experiences of others who have been there before, how the Realization that we want something more out of life is the event that triggers the blooming process.

Wanting more out of life is a powerful motivator. When we finally reach the point that we admit that we want more— and are committed to achieving more—we will manage to overcome those obstacles that have been preventing us from attaining our dreams. I'm not suggesting that all we have to do is close our eyes, make a wish, and all detours and roadblocks will disappear. The late bloomers you will meet in this book will testify that the fulfillment of dreams requires planning and hard work. But they also will tell you that the knowledge that you are working toward the *right* dream can be as satisfying as achieving the dream itself. Roadblocks and detours always will be there, but the personal satisfaction derived from pursuing your own dream will give you the strength to transcend them or the ingenuity to accommodate them or the patience to wait them out. The lesson to be learned from these late bloomers is simply this: We all have the power to be what we want to be once we realize what that is and dedicate ourselves to becoming it.

Charles Dutton didn't know he wanted more until he was in prison, serving time for homicide, among other offenses. Charles was born in Baltimore and was raised in a housing project there. His parents separated when he was three. His father, a truckdriver, was rarely in town. His mother, a florist, struggled to feed her family and raise her three children. In his early years Charles was bright but difficult for his mother to control. By age twelve, he says, he was "incorrigible."

"I was more interested in what was going on on the street corner than in the classroom," he recalled.

Charles looked up to the tough, older guys who would gather on the street, drinking and bragging about their profitable lives of crime. Much to his mother's despair, he fell in with a bad crowd. He quit school in the eighth grade because he couldn't stand being confined to a classroom or being told what to do.

In his youth, Charles was an amateur boxer of some talent. He now believes that if he had been more disciplined, he could have pursued a professional boxing career. "Boxing is a very demanding sport. It requires time and a great deal of training. I wasn't willing to make the commitment back then," he explained.

Charles isn't sure why he turned out the way he did. All he knows is that violence was a way of life in his rough, crime-ridden neighborhood. "When I was growing up, I'd watch a report on Vietnam on the news and I'd think, I feel like I'm living in Vietnam. Every weekend, you'd hear shots all night long. You'd hear the screeching of the ambulance sirens. You'd see the blood. I knew people who would kill someone on a Friday night and be out on bail bragging about it on Saturday."

When he was seventeen, Charles got into a fight with a neighborhood tough. Charles stabbed him. "He would have killed me if he had the chance," he said. The youth died four months later.

Charles was sentenced to eighteen months in prison. "As long as a black is killing another black, it's not regarded as any big deal," he said matter-of-factly. After seven months he was paroled. Five months later, he was convicted of possessing a gun. He was sentenced to three years.

The violence Charles knew in the streets was nothing compared to what he found behind bars. Tensions were heightened by the political waves washing across the country during the late sixties. On the outside radical black groups such as the Black Panthers were indicting racist America and preaching revolution. On the inside they were urging "political prisoners" to revolt. Charles said that, like many of his fellow inmates, he was ready to die for "the cause."

By his own admission, he was a "tough" inmate who couldn't seem to keep out of trouble. When his three years were almost up, Charles acted as a ringleader in a prison riot. As his punishment eight more years were tacked on to his sentence.

Charles had very little interest in any of the organized activities the prison offered. He refused to work in the metal shop or in the kitchen. The only activity that he enjoyed was reading. He checked book after book out of the prison library. By chance, he stumbled upon his first play, Douglas Turner Ward's *Day of Absence*. A satire that takes place in a southern town, it is performed by black actors in whiteface. Intrigued by the play, Charles decided that it would be perfect for the prisoners to put on themselves. Charles had no trouble finding eight other inmates to join an acting group.

"There was a lot of energy and raw talent in the prison," he said. "The acting group gave them a chance to release some of that energy in a constructive way."

But to Charles, the group was much more than a distraction from prison life. From the first moment that he read aloud from the script, he sensed that there was something special happening. He seemed to have a natural gift for performing. He didn't know where it came from or why it had suddenly surfaced. All he knew was that there were emotions stirring inside him that he had never felt before. "I felt that there was something almost sacred about acting," he explained. "I knew right away that this was what I had been meant to do."

Fascinated by the theater, Charles wanted to learn as much as he could. Slowly, paying attention to detail, he struggled through Shakespeare's *King Lear*, finding it the most moving experience of his life.

Although Charles loved acting, it never occurred to him that he could become an actor. In fact, he hardly gave any thought at all to what he would do when and if he ever got out of prison, and because of the way things were going, it looked like he never would. At twenty-two, Charles experienced the Realization that would change his view of life. During a squabble with another prisoner, he was stabbed in the neck with an ice pick. He nearly died from the attack. "It was an incredible shock. I had never been hurt so badly in my entire life," he admitted.

Charles spent the next few months recovering in the

prison infirmary. He knew that as soon as he was healed, everyone would expect him to seek his revenge—an eye for an eye being the prison code. Many of his buddies in prison were friends from his old neighborhood. They were bonded by violence, swearing from the time they were teenagers that they would die and go to hell together. Charles, who was considered one of the toughest in the group, had a reputation to uphold. "It was the most intense pressure that I had ever experienced. I had known many of the guys since I was eight or nine. They looked up to me."

Charles was confronted with the most difficult decision of his life. He felt compelled to punish his assailant. And yet, if he did, he would undoubtedly get a longer prison sentence. Of course, that wouldn't be the end of it. Then it would be up to the other inmate to seek his revenge on Charles, and the cycle of violence would continue. He might even be killed.

For the first time, Charles took stock of his life, thinking about where he came from and where he was going. "I finally decided, it's my life, I don't have to answer to anybody. I realized that all those guys I used to look up to, where were they now? At forty or fifty, many of them weren't around anymore. They were either dead or they were still doing the same thing, hanging out on the street corner, drinking the bottle of wine. They may have grown older, but they're still fighting. I said to myself, 'What stupidity, what wasted lives.'"

After much agonizing, Charles decided not to seek his revenge. His old friends cut him off. Charles became a loner, spending his days by himself in his cell, reading plays and pondering his future. Having severed his ties with his old life, he needed to build a new life for himself. He turned to the one thing that had given his life special meaning, that had given him a sense of who he was and who he wanted to be. Charles decided to become an actor.

"I wanted to act more than I had ever wanted anything else in my life," he explained in a quiet, emotional voice.

To most of us, the obstacles that he had to overcome would have seemed insurmountable. He had six more years to serve, little education, and no prospects. But his dream of becoming an actor kept him going. "I made a commitment to do it," he said. "I realized that having something to believe in is the essence of being on this earth. There's something almost divine and spiritual when you leave negative things and find something positive to live for."

Charles requested permission to participate in the prison high-school-equivalency program. At first, the prison officials were skeptical, never expecting an inmate with his kind of record to stick it out. But he did. A hard worker, he completed high school, earning the privilege to take courses outside the prison at a nearby community college. Impressed by his progress, the parole board released Charles early in 1976.

On a partial scholarship, Charles enrolled in Towson State University in Maryland to study acting. On the first day of registration, he was devastated to learn that the theater program was already filled. Refusing to take no for an answer, he called Paul Berman, a well-known director who was then chairman of the department, to plead his case. After hearing his story, Berman made room for one more student.

At Towson a new world opened up to Charles. Studying everything from classical theater to the avant garde, he thrived in his new environment. Charles did not aspire to be a star. In fact, he assumed that he would spend the rest of his life working in local theater. Paul Berman had other ideas for his prized student. After graduation he suggested to Charles that he apply for a scholarship at the Yale Drama School. Although he didn't think that there would be much of a chance that Yale would accept an ex-convict, Charles applied anyway.

In fall 1981, Charles auditioned at Yale, performing a soliloquy from *Macbeth* and the part of Lenny in *Of Mice and Men*. Although his performances were well received, he remained extremely skeptical about his chances of being accepted.

Much to his amazement the following April he received a letter from Yale offering him a full scholarship for the following fall. Charles, overtaken by a classic case of "success anxiety," didn't venture outside his apartment for the next three days, for fear that something terrible was going to happen that would prevent him from fulfilling his dream. Eventually he calmed down, but he knew that his life would never be the same.

Yale did change Charles's life: He was transformed from a talented, aspiring performer into a professional actor. Although the program was extremely demanding, Charles found it to be the "greatest theatrical experience of a lifetime. Everybody was a professional, trying to do the best they could whether they were working in the front office, on stage, or backstage."

When the Yale Repertory Company decided to perform the work of a new playwright, August Wilson, Charles auditioned for a part in his play, *Ma Rainey's Black Bottom*. A hit in New Haven, the play opened on Broadway in 1984.

That's what late bloomer Charles Dutton did. When he

decided that he wanted something more, his life was at a dead end. Many people in his situation would have been crippled by hopelessness and despair. And yet, like so many other late bloomers, Charles was able to transform negative feelings into the positive energy necessary to alter his destiny.

At thirty-four years old, Charles is on Broadway playing the role of Levee, a black trumpet player in *Ma Rainey's Black Bottom*. Set in a Chicago recording studio in 1927, *Ma Rainey's* deals with the friction between a blues singer and her four-man band and the white owners of a record company. When the play debuted in New York in October 1984, Dutton received extraordinary reviews, praising his performance as "red-hot" and "magnificent." *The New York Times* recently referred to him as "one of the season's most talked about actors." In 1985, Dutton was nominated for a Tony award.

"From jail to Yale," as Charles jokingly refers to his arduous journey from prison to the Broadway stage, was a road filled with problems and pitfalls. From the lowest point in his life, Charles had to choose between two paths. In the short run, the easy way out would have been to seek his revenge on the other inmate, thus enhancing his reputation as a tough prisoner. If he had followed his old pattern, he would have been accepting a life of violence that would have probably led to his own destruction. But Charles wanted more out of life. He had found something else to believe in, something that was more powerful than peer pressure or his own desire to avenge a wrong. Through acting, Charles had discovered a constructive, creative part of himself that made him see that life could be worth living. His dream gave him the power to say "This is my life and I'm going to do what's best for me." Although it took a great deal of courage to change the course of his life, as Charles observed, when we finally find something positive to believe in, we tap into inner sources of strength that we never even knew existed.

Charles believes that acting is his true calling, the vocation that makes him feel as if "I'm finally doing what I was born to do."

None of us would accuse Charles Dutton of being self-centered, selfish, or a product of the "Me Generation." Yet he did exactly what all of us want to do but frequently stop ourselves from doing for fear of being labeled overly ambitious or narcissistic. He sought fulfillment by finally recognizing that he wanted more out of life and was entitled to it.

It's important for us to realize that our attitudes about self-fulfillment change about as frequently as the length of women's hemlines. There have been times in our recent history when it was very much in vogue to "do your own thing," when the quest for self-fulfillment was considered a lofty pursuit. And there have been times when economic and other pressures have made even the desire for self-fulfillment seem frivolous. And there have been times when the proponents of both points of view collided head-on with each other. For example, when I was growing up, I used to accuse my parents of having "Depression mentality." By that I meant that I thought that they had displayed some of the personality quirks associated with survivors of that economic catastrophe. It meant having a pessimistic view of life. Victims of the Depression, who had experienced more disappointments during those few years than most of us ever will in our lifetimes, were extremely cautious and security minded. They saved instead of investing. If they did not have cash, they did without. And though they had very little, they deem themselves fortunate to have had anything at all. My father is a case in point. An accountant—and a good one at that—he labored for four decades in a profession he utterly despised. When I asked him why he never considered switching careers (in fact he would have preferred to be a teacher or a sociologist), he looked at me with disbelief. Switching careers in search of self-fulfillment would have been irresponsible, not to mention "impossible." His children—my brother (a medical researcher who lives from grant to grant and declines to practice medicine) and I—view things differently. For us a paycheck is not sufficient compensation for our labors. We want—and are willing to work for—psychic income as well.

Why did the apples fall so far from the tree? One reason is the tree itself. Men like my father spent their psyches to buy security not only for themselves but for their children. As a result, we greet our futures with great expectations. Untouched by an experience as daunting as the Depression, we simply take it for granted that we will be able to earn a living. For us the challenge is not finding a job but finding the right job.

Another reason is the social and political currents and crosscurrents that have washed across America in the past two decades, carrying new values and attitudes.

Once upon a time there were the 1950s, when many of us led lives of quiet, comfortable conformity. Our parents, the children of the Depression, zealously pursued an American Dream epitomized by a house in suburbia, a wood-paneled station wagon, kids, dogs, and weekends at the country club. The Cold War and McCarthyism had cooled political dissent. Intellectuals such as Adlai Stevenson were "out." We marched together to a miraculous if materialistic tune.

In the mid-1960s our idyll was shattered by the "youth movement," when the sons and daughters of affluence challenged—and worse, ridiculed—the values and life-styles of their parents. College campuses from Berkeley to Columbia erupted in protests over the Vietnam war, civil rights, and student power. The generation that had been raised by the man in the gray flannel suit put on bell-bottoms and body paint. But the rebellion was more than skin deep. It touched the soul of a nation.

What we were saying—what was so difficult for our parents to swallow—was that we did not want to live the kinds of lives that they had wished for us. We wanted something more. Determined to conquer the world on our own terms, we were not going to let things like mortgage payments or car loans hold us back. Parents who had scrimped and sacrificed to secure their children's future were stunned by the ingratitude of a generation, but, as time went by and expressions such as "do your own thing" and "whatever turns you on" entered the lexicon, many of these same parents were provoked to examine, perhaps for the first time, their lives. Businessmen who had devoted their lives to material pursuits became intrigued by the spiritual. Husbands and wives who had married young became enchanted by the sexual revolution. Seemingly successful individuals who were inexplicably unhappy with their lives began to wonder whether, after all, the kids were on to something.

Goals and values were reexamined. Some were discarded; others were packed away. Depression mentality was out. Risk taking was in. A well-known game show, "Let's Make a Deal," was founded on the premise that fifty bucks in the hand couldn't be worth more than what's behind the secret door. Magazines and newspapers were filled with tales of people trying to "find themselves"—often at great personal cost to themselves and their families. And they looked everywhere. Stockbrokers "dropped out" of the rat race to live off the land in Vermont. Housewives walked out on families to hitchhike cross-country. Students left colleges to live on pig farms in New Mexico.

Such incidents characterized what has become known as the "human potential movement," which swept the country in the 1970s. As its name implies, this movement was based on the belief that if we made a conscious effort to change and grow, we could achieve unimagined heights. The belief that each of us has a vast, untapped potential is in part based on the work of Abraham Maslow, a leading twentieth-century psychologist who is credited with first coining the terms *peak experience* and *self-actualization*. Maslow studied a group of men and women whom he felt were remarkable people to see what attributes or experiences they all shared. From his research he derived a profile of what he called a "self-actualizing person." Much of Maslow's description is complicated, sometimes bordering on the mystical. Some for the more mundane aspects of self-actualization can be defined through work. According to Maslow, self-actualizing people are involved in work that they love, a "vocation in the old sense, a priestly sense." They are independent— they are not slaves to authority—but at the same time they manage to be giving and loving. Many people may strive for self-actualization, but few people actually achieve it.

As the theories of Maslow and other psychologists became popularized, many of us began to seek out ways to fulfill our potential. We turned to self-help books, such as *I'm*

OK, You're OK, and *How to Be Your Own Best Friend*. We flocked to encounter groups and consciousness-raising sessions to get in touch with our feelings. Therapy, once considered only a necessity for the sick and a luxury for the rich, was now becoming a middle-class pastime. An entire era was devoted to the notion of "more." As psychologist Arlene Kagle has said, "If anything in your life—your marriage, your children, your job, your figure—was less than ideal, the prevailing belief was that you could rid yourself of what you had and find 'more.'"

Cries for "more" were heard everywhere. There's got to be more to life than simply being a money machine, said men who up until then had kept their lives of quiet desperation to themselves. Women, especially those who had grown up in the preliberation days, also clamored for "more." In her excellent study of mid-life women, *Women of a Certain Age*, psychologist Lillian Rubin described one homemaker who after spending twenty years with "kids, doctors, and the PTA" finally said, "There's got to be more to life than hot flashes and headaches."

We didn't always find what we were looking for. Sometimes, in pursuit of more, we ended up with less. Many of us bailed out of marriages only to find that the world could be a lonely and cold place. Some of us embarked on long journeys to find ourselves only to get hopelessly lost on the way back. Some of us dropped out of schools or careers only to discover that we had made an unnecessary detour.

Many of us, though, did find something better. By taking a more critical view of our relationships, we improved our marriages and enriched our lives. By leaving a career that we found deadening, we found a new life through another vocation. By dropping out of school, we gave ourselves the time to figure out what it was we really wanted, not what somebody else wanted for us.

For many of us, the quest is not over. We are still searching for more. Although the human potential movement is now as dated as granny glasses or Peter Max posters, the philosophy of the movement is as relevant as ever. It has changed the way we think, not just the way some of us think but the way most of us think. Consider the following: In the late 1970s public-opinion researcher Daniel Yankelovich discovered that nearly three-quarters of all Americans spent a great deal of time thinking about themselves and their inner lives, "this in a nation once notorious for its impatience with inwardness." Another recent national study revealed that Americans were not only more "inward-looking" than in the past, but that we actually have a more positive view of ourselves. What all this means is that we have become more aware of our psychological needs and, consequently, more concerned about our own self-fulfillment.

Not everyone views this as a positive trend. Inevitably words such as *selfish* and *self-centered* are used to describe our new self-awareness. Writer Tom Wolfe, who dubbed the 1970s the "Me Decade," distilled the entire human potential movement down to one phrase, "Let's talk about me." In a stinging indictment of the quest for self-realization, Wolfe accused Americans of becoming so obsessed with self—self-awareness, self-improvement, self-importance—that we were in danger of losing the traditional spirit of dedication and self-sacrifice that motivated one generation to strive to leave the world a better place for the next.

No one escaped Wolfe's wrath. He condemned feminists, therapists, Madison Avenue copywriters, and "wife shuckers" for constantly thinking of "me, me, me" to the exclusion of anyone else.

An equally grim view of the Me Generation is depicted in Christopher Lasch's *The Culture of Narcissism*, in which he presents a chilling portrait of a society consisting of individuals solely out for themselves. According to Lasch, the increase in self-absorption is due to a vacuum created by a breakdown in our traditional values—respect for family, religion, the work ethic, and responsibility to community. Lasch contends that as we move away from these traditional values, we are desperately searching for something in their place to give our lives meaning. Whereas in the past we may have sought guidance from our parents, the village elder, or the parish priest, today we seek solace from psychologists who encourage us to focus on our needs and desires.

But before we begin beating our chests, I think it's important to point out that late bloomers are the last people who need a sermon on self-sacrifice. Most often late bloomers have put the needs of others above their own. They are fathers who put their personal dreams on hold so they can support their families. They are mothers who leave jobs that they love to answer the call of another equally compelling dream—to care for their newborn infants. They are dutiful sons who carry out their parents' wishes without regard to their own. They are daughters who were tracked into marriage and motherhood before they could find out who they were or what they wanted. They are caring, responsible people who after years of deferring their personal desires reach the point where they must finally cry out, "I want something more."

Late bloomers are not selfish or narcissistic or wrapped up in themselves. In fact, self-centeredness—living only "for me"—can prevent us from blooming. To grow we need supportive, honest, and giving relationships. The people in our lives—mentors, role models, lovers, friends, and spouses—are often instrumental in helping us bloom.

While self-centeredness can ultimately be self-destructive, excessive selflessness can be equally crippling. For many of us the challenge is finding the middle ground where we can balance our needs against the needs of those who are important to us. Sometimes we have to make sacrifices, and sometimes we have to call upon others to sacrifice. It should work both ways, but especially for many women it is a one-way proposition. They give, and others take. Deferring emotional needs has become second nature to women. The rise of feminism over the past fifteen years has made us aware of this problem, but it has not offered very many solutions.

It's still very difficult for many women to ask the question "Whose life is it anyway?" because the answer may be too depressing. Their lives are not their own. Very often their time is divided among children, husbands, and sometimes even elderly parents, with very little left for themselves. There are times when we all—men and women—have to make sacrifices for the good of others. But it's not healthy always to place ourselves at the bottom of the list. Psychologist Carol Gilligan, author of *In A Different Voice*, asserts that in order for women to develop a sense of self-esteem, they must believe that their needs are at least as important as everybody else's. She's not saying that women have to be selfish all the time, only that women have to think of themselves some of the time.

Women may nod their heads knowingly at Dr. Gilligan's advice, but for many of them it is not very easy to follow. Despite gains made by the women's movement, most of the responsibility of caring for children and maintaining a household falls on women, whether or not they work outside the home. Very often they are torn in so many different directions that they don't have a lot of time to think about self-fulfillment, let alone do anything about it.

The tendency of some women to defer seeking fulfillment so they can fulfill the needs of others is only one reason why so many turn out to be late bloomers. There are other factors that slow down progress. For one thing, many women have a great deal of difficulty forming goals, which I believe is a reflection of upbringing. From interviews with late bloomers, I detected a major difference between men and women in terms of childhood experiences. Many of the men I spoke with noted that when they were very young they were tracked into the wrong careers by overzealous parents who believed that they were doing the right thing for their sons. Most of the women I interviewed had just the opposite experience: They were not tracked into any careers at all. Most of them grew up in homes where the possibility that they might have to work was never even discussed. As girls, a few had the usual daydreams about becoming models or movie stars but hardly any had given serious thought to their adult lives. Their parents expected them to be wives and mothers, which is what they became.

Women were—and I think to an extent still are—expected to find fulfillment in the home. Some of them are able to focus their talents and energies on homemaking, deriving great satisfaction from their labors. Others are not. They may start out believing that love alone is enough to sustain them, only to find that their lives are lacking and they want something more.

Patricia Ferrari can remember the exact moment that she had the Realization that forced her to change the direction of her life. Hers is a story with which any homemaker— whether she is happy or frustrated or a little bit of both— can identify.

One evening, after a particularly hectic day of feeding, chasing, and cleaning up after her three children—all under age five—something snapped. When her husband, Robert, a lawyer, came home for dinner, Patricia did something that she had never done before. She announced she was going out for a walk, leaving her bewildered husband and children to fend for themselves.

"I wound up at a movie," she recalled. "I was simply exhausted, and walking out was my way of asking for attention."

By the time Patricia returned home later that evening, Robert had wisked the children off to his parents' house so that he and his wife could have dinner alone at a favorite local restaurant. At first Patricia was embarrassed by the incident. "It was as if I had admitted that I couldn't cope," she said. After talking with her husband over a leisurely dinner, Patricia realized that she was suffering from much more than a temporary case of housewife blues. "I kept saying, 'Let's take a vacation, let's go places, let's do things together,' and Bob said, 'I don't know what you're going to do, but I have to go back to work.' I realized then that my underlying plea was 'take me places, keep me company, entertain me.' I didn't know what to do with myself."

Patricia realized something else that night: As much as she loved her children, there were only so many hours a day she could devote to motherhood without losing her sanity. "I knew that unless I found something else to add to my life, I would always be looking for someone else to entertain me."

Seeing Patricia in her impressive law office on the thirty-third floor of a New York City skyscraper, it is hard to imagine this confident, professional woman as a harried homemaker. But that's what she was, fifteen years ago when, she says, she finally accepted responsibility for her life and started on that long road from motherhood to a partnership at a top law firm. Patricia didn't rush out the day after that fateful evening and enroll in law school. That's not her style. During what she calls the "gestation period," Patricia, a thoughtful, intelligent woman, mulled over her future. She didn't know what she was going to do, all she did know was that eventually she was going to do *something*.

Back when she was an undergraduate at St. Joseph's College in Hartford, Connecticut, Patricia had briefly toyed with the idea of going to law school but quickly dismissed it. "I found obstacles. I kept saying I couldn't afford to go, but that wasn't the real reason. I guess I just didn't want it badly enough," she admitted. Instead she studied merchandising, not because of any strong interest in retailing but because she simply didn't know what else to do.

During Thanksgiving weekend of her senior year, she met Robert Ferrari, eight years her senior, who was an established New York lawyer. The following spring they were engaged. Patricia remembers feeling a rush of pride as classmates gathered around her on graduation day to admire her ring. "Now it sounds funny, but friends at school were giving me accolades. I now realize that they were saying 'Congratulations, a ring for graduation.'"

Robert and Patricia were married the following Thanksgiving weekend, a year to the day after they met. Eleven months later Patricia quit her job as an assistant buyer at Sears to care for their newborn daughter, Lisa. Three other children followed in rapid succession. At first Patricia was perfectly content to be a wife and mother. "Women were supposed to get married and have children. It never occurred to me that I might want to make a deliberate choice in another direction. I just wasn't motivated toward a goal," she explained.

Throughout their marriage Patricia and Robert frequently discussed his cases. In fact, Robert was so impressed with his wife's cool, logical approach to legal problems that he often told her that she would make a great lawyer. Soon it became an accepted fact that one day, perhaps when the kids were grown and out of the house, Patricia would go to law school. After the birth of her fourth child, Patricia mentioned her long-range plan to her mother. Much to her daugher's chagrin, her normally positive, supportive mother quickly replied. "No, you won't." Patricia looked at her indignantly and said, "What do you mean, I won't? Of course, I'm going to go to law school. I'm just waiting for the kids to graduate from high school." At that point, her mother pointed out that she and Robert would be so strapped putting four children through college, they wouldn't have any money left for her law school tuition.

"It was just a passing comment," Patricia recalled. "But I was forced to face the truth for a moment. She was right."

A few months later, on a cold February night, Robert came home early one night from work. Before even taking off his coat, he walked into the kitchen to discuss a legal problem with his wife. As Patricia cooked spaghetti and her youngest daughter, Rachel, crawled on the kitchen floor, the couple debated a particular point of law. "You know, you really should go to law school," Robert told his wife for the countless time in their marriage.

Patricia responded to her husband's statement with a simple "I know." To this day, Patricia isn't exactly sure why she answered the way she did. Maybe her mother's comment a few months earlier had had a deeper effect than she had realized. Or maybe some internal clock had finally signaled that it was the right time for her to make her move. Within five minutes Patricia and Robert were getting down to details, discussing to which school she would apply and who would baby-sit for the children. Since they couldn't afford a full-time housekeeper, Patricia decided to go to school at night.

The next week Patricia frantically picked up applications from local law schools and arranged to take the LSATs, the mandatory law school admissions test. A few weeks later, she left home early one Saturday morning to take the day-long exam at New York University Law School. When she emerged from the redbrick building at 5:00 P.M., she saw her husband and four children standing across the street, leaning on a fence outside Washington Square Park. Upon seeing her mother, one of her children called out excitedly, "Mommy, are you a lawyer yet?"

"Everyone laughed. It really broke the tension," Patricia recalled with a big smile.

Finding a law school that would accept a mother of four who had been out of school for eight years—and who was applying late—was no easy feat. During one admissions interview, the dean of Fordham Law School scanned Patricia's college transcript and suggested that she first get a master's degree before attempting to take on the study of law. Patricia held her ground. "I told him I didn't want a master's, that I wanted a law degree. I remember saying with real passion, 'I'm twenty-nine years old. If I don't do it now, I'll never do it.'"

Somehow Patricia must have conveyed her deep motivation and sense of urgency because by fall she was a student at Fordham Law School.

After her first month at school, Patricia discovered that she was pregnant. For the first time in her life, she was scared. "During the whole summer, everyone had been asking me how I was going to manage school with four babies. Our oldest was seven at that point. When I found that I was pregnant, I remember coming home and sitting there talking to Bob. I was feeling very overwhelmed by the work load. I talked about postponing school, but he said if I dropped out now, I would never return. Then he told me to 'take it one day at a time.' Those words seemed to have a hypnotic effect on me. I never talked about quitting again," Patricia said.

The four years that followed were rough on Patricia and her family. By late afternoon before an exam or an important class, Patricia would be watching the clock, praying that the baby-sitter would show up. Weekends were spent studying, and every free second was devoted to the children. Fortunately, her family was very supportive. If the baby-sitter got sick or a child needed to be rushed to the hospital, Patricia's mother would show at the door to help. And during the entire pressure-filled four years, Robert never complained about his wife's hectic schedule.

The continual tug-of-war between family responsibilities and schoolwork and the seemingly endless papers to write and briefs to read could not dampen the thrill Patricia felt each time she walked into Fordham. "To me, being a lawyer is much more than a way to earn a living," she said, her voice filled with emotion. "My family always had a tremendous amount of respect for lawyers. I wasn't looking for prestige as much as a sense of achievement."

The four years didn't exactly fly by, but Patricia made it through law school and did well enough so that after graduation she landed a part-time job with a top Wall Street law firm. She left a few years later to pursue a matrimonial practice with Phillips, Nizer, Benjamin, Krim & Ballon, a leading New York firm, where she has been made a partner.

Once again, from Patricia's story we see how empowering the Realization can be. When she decided that she could not find fulfillment through her family alone—that she wanted more, for the first time in her life, she began to think seriously about forming a career goal. After she choose her goal, a difficult one at that, she redirected some of her energy away from her family and focused it on her dream.

Patricia is the first to recognize the irony of her story. The twenty-one-year-old undergraduate who was overwhelmed by the thought of law school was put to shame by the twenty-nine-year-old mother of five who let nothing stand in her way. "It's timing," she explained. "When you are really ready to do something, you will find a way and the means to do it."

It's ironic that for many women like Patricia, the search for self-fulfillment leads them to a competitive, predominantly male business world from which women previously were excluded. Yet many men who are locked into high-pressure jobs feel trapped in their world. They are prisoners of success, working to support a life-style to which they and their families have grown accustomed. The point is that in an ideal world we would all be free to choose careers that we find exciting and interesting. We would not be pushed into jobs on the basis of sex-role stereotyping, economic need, or any consideration apart from desire and aptitude.

I doubt that I'm bursting anyone's balloon by saying that we do not live in an ideal world. Many of us have jobs we feel ambivalent about at best. Many of us actually hate our jobs. In his book *Working*, Studs Terkel revealed how few people derive any pleasure whatsoever from the activity that occupies most of their waking hours. He told the story of a twenty-four-year-old receptionist who cried every morning because she didn't want to report to a job she found tedious and demeaning. He also introduced us to the short-haul truckdriver who complained that his job was giving him chronic indigestion. And he showed us the New York stockbroker who believed that his job had no value whatsoever either to society or himself.

Why, then, do so many of us stay in jobs that we find utterly boring, stressful, or degrading? Some of us are "stuck," because although we know what we don't want we haven't the foggiest notion of what we do want. So we stay put. Some of us are fearful that if we start looking for something better, we'll end up with something worse—or with nothing. So we stay put. But then there are those of us who have made a conscious and deliberate decision to sacrifice our happiness for economic gain. We stay in jobs we don't like because they offer financial security.

All of us are forced to make choices and accept trade-offs at various times. We may have dreams—creative dreams that may not pay off in the short run, impractical dreams that may never pay off. If we decide to pursue money over everything else, we must sacrifice our emotional needs for our financial desires. We no longer have the freedom to select the career that offers the greatest enjoyment and fulfillment. We look for the job that offers the biggest bucks. For some of us, being well paid is compensation enough for doing something that we don't particularly enjoy. We may have perks such as a company car, a prestigious title that wows them at the country club, or an expense account that goes a long way in soothing our troubled souls. But for many of us, it is not enough. Although we are reluctant to admit it, deep down inside we're miserable.

There may come a time when we can no longer stifle our feelings of pain and frustration. First, we look for a quick fix—we go on a vacation or buy ourselves a new, expensive toy. When that doesn't work, we begin searching for a cure. We look for something that will bring us back to life, that will give us a sense of meaning and purpose. As we will learn from late bloomer Martin Boris, when we finally find what we're looking for we can never go back.

When he was twenty, Martin, a premed student, graduated from New York University with a straight-A average, the highest academic honors, and a pile of rejection letters from every medical school to which he applied. It was 1951, the height of the McCarthy era. A political activist who by his own admission "signed every petition and marched in every protest," Martin managed to get himself blacklisted. Despite his high grades, no medical school would accept him, which forced him to abandon his lifetime dream of becoming a doctor.

Born during the Great Depression, Martin, like many of his contemporaries, was used to disappointment. His father, who owned a chicken farm in upstate New York, struggled to support his family. Earning a living was life's major challenge; any notions of self-fulfillment were irrelevant. *Any* career would do as long as it provided food for the family.

At age twenty-two Martin married Gloria, his college girlfriend, an elementary-school teacher. He decided to stay at NYU to pursue a graduate degree in English so he could eventually teach at the college level. While he attended classes, he worked part-time in a jewelry factory on the Lower East Side. Once again graduating with straight As, Martin was offered a part-time job as an instructor at NYU. Martin then realized the grim realities of academia: It would take years to earn a full professorship, and even then it wouldn't pay enough to support a family. Since he had some experience in jewelry manufacturing, Martin decided to scrape together enough money to open his own small jewelry business. Although he worked long hours, he could barely earn a living because American jewelers were being clobbered by the cheap and plentiful Japanese imports. Martin assessed his situation. He was in his midtwenties and had already failed at three careers. What was he going to do next?

A practical man, Martin didn't waste too much time anguishing over this decision. He simply reviewed his talents and his likes and dislikes and came up with three possible careers: florist, pharmacist, and optometrist. He wrote the three choices on a piece of paper and pasted it on a dart board over his desk. The dart landed on the *h* in pharmacist.

Much to his surprise, Martin actually enjoyed pharmaceutical college, completing four years of course work in three. Upon graduation, he and a fellow classmate invested their life savings to purchase a drugstore on a busy Queens street. That same year Gloria quit her job to care for their newborn daughter, Elizabeth. Within seven years they had three children.

The drugstore proved to be so successful that Martin and his partner soon bought another store. When that one took off, they bought five more. Martin, the comptroller of the mini-chain, became obsessed with the day-to-day operations of the stores. "I would find myself getting up at four in the morning in a cold sweat wondering if the check I had issued to the government was going to clear, whether the special sale that I set up would occur on a weekend of torrential rain," he recalled.

For nearly twenty years, he worked seven days a week, often for sixteen hours a day. When he reached his early forties, his wife became aware of the fact that he was nearing a nervous breakdown. "Here I was, running from store to store, putting out all the fires, handling the paperwork, solving all of the problems. My wife kept telling me I needed a vacation, that I had to slow down."

During this period Martin spent a great deal of time reflecting on his life. He had "made it" in the conventional sense of the term: He had become an extremely prosperous man who lived in a lovely house in an affluent suburb, who could give his wife and children everything that they had ever wanted or needed. Martin had fulfilled the American Dream, and yet he himself felt very unfulfilled. The work that he had once found exciting and challenging now seemed dull and flat. It wasn't just boredom—he could have lived with that. But Martin felt as if he was being consumed by an "emotional cancer," and he didn't know what to do about it.

From the depths of despair, Martin reached the Realization that there was more to life than simply making money and that he wanted to find what that something more was. At forty-four years old, Martin made a major decision. He would take Sundays off.

On the first few Sundays he took off, Martin did absolutely nothing. Within a month, however, after he felt more bored than relaxed, he began searching for new ways to spend his free day. Having just completed *Lust for Life*, Irving Stone's biography of van Gogh, Martin decided to take up painting. With great zeal, he purchased an easel, a set of paints, and a supply of canvas. He spent several Sundays painting from dawn till dusk until he realized that he had neither the interest nor the talent for art. Quietly he stashed his art supplies in the basement and continued his quest for some meaningful activity. Although it didn't work out, Martin looks back on this experiment as an important turning point. "It got me off square one," he explained. "I was groping for something. By taking that first step, it opened me up to the possibility that I can make changes in my life."

His second endeavor paid off in more ways than one. On one of his free Sundays, he entered a writing contest sponsored by a trade magazine. In an article called "Détente," he humorously described his twenty-one-year relationship with his business partner. He was elated when he won the first prize of one hundred dollars.

Buoyed by his success, Martin decided to write a novel in the hopes of becoming a professional writer. Every spare moment was spent thrashing out the details of his story involving an affair between a middle-aged Long Island doctor and his gardener's wife. As he began to reduce his time in the stores to concentrate on his writing, he discovered a feeling of fulfillment from work that he had never experienced before. Martin knew that he could never return to his old life.

Although he was financially secure, it was still a big decision for Martin to sell his share of the business to write full-time at home. For one thing, his wife needed convincing that he wasn't having a nervous breakdown. After all, Martin, the dependable workaholic, had never done anything like this before in his life. For another thing, Martin had fairly traditional notions about what men were supposed to do, and men were supposed to go to work every day.

But his desire to write transcended any reservations he or his family may have had. Martin threw himself into his work, completing his book within a year. He was about to send his manuscript off to a publisher when a friend, who had been a writer for several years, advised him to get an agent. That sounded easy enough, so Martin sent letters describing his book to a dozen literary agents. In each case, he received a form letter explaining that they did not handle the works of unpublished writers.

Martin's hopes soared when he saw an article in *The New York Times* quoting a literary agent who was complaining about the lack of novels set in Long Island. Martin quickly sent the agent a note describing his book only to receive the same rejection letter. Angered by the response, he wrote a funny but pointed letter to the reporter who wrote the story. The next day the reporter called and apologetically asked how he could make amends. Martin quickly replied, "Read my book."

The reporter did better than that. He hand-delivered the manuscript to the agent. After reviewing it the agent showed the book to a few publishers. Within a few months, Martin had a contract from a major publisher and a substantial paperback sale.

Martin's book, *Two + Two*, received excellent reviews. A Hollywood studio hired a well-known writer to work on the screenplay. Although the movie deal fell through, Martin was not disheartened. "I've got to keep going. I've got novels cooking in the back of my head to last for the next three hundred fifty years," he said.

From Martin's story we can see how a mid-life career change precipitated by the desire for something more can lead to a sense of renewal and purpose. Almost overnight Martin was transformed from a man who had lost his zest for living to someone who looked forward to each new day as another opportunity to write. Life for Martin became exciting and challenging.

The changes Martin made to accommodate his need for fulfillment reflect society's changing attitudes toward work. When Martin began his career in the 1950s, the work ethic of an honest day's work for an honest day's pay prevailed. But as we became more concerned about improving the quality of our lives, work took on a new dimension. Like Martin, many of us searched for something that would offer spiritual satisfaction as well as monetary income. Martin found what he was looking for, and although he may never earn as much money as a writer as he did as a pharmacist, he is happier than he has ever been in his entire life.

As in Martin's case, many of us begin the blooming process knowing that we want more out of life without knowing precisely what "more" is. We know that something is missing, but we don't know what. But as we have seen in this chapter, negative feelings of frustration and discontent can trigger some very positive changes. It's only after we "bottom out"—reach our level of unhappiness—that we start to take life-affirming action that turns our lives around.

The Realization that we want more out of life is a critical stage in blooming, but it is just the first step. If we want more but do nothing about it, we will remain nipped in the bud. But if we make a commitment to strive toward all that we are capable of achieving, we will find what we are seeking.

CHAPTER 3

Dreams vs. Pipe Dreams

*T*hroughout our lives many of us have dreams about what we want to do and who we want to be. There may be obstacles—self-imposed roadblocks, as well as those hurled in our path by fate and circumstance—that prevent us from achieving many of these dreams. As the years fly by, we may get panicky, discouraged, and even depressed if we are not living up to our expectations. But as we will learn from the stories of late bloomers, putting a dream on hold doesn't mean that we are putting it out of our lives forever. When the time is right, we will resurrect these dreams and, one by one, jump the hurdles that are blocking their fulfillment.

We may nurture many different dreams simultaneously. Our personal dreams involve our own self-fulfillment. But we may also have dreams that are intertwined with the destinies of others. We may, for example, dream about the kinds of lives we wish for our spouses and our children. Some of us may be deeply committed to an ideal — a vision of the way we feel the world should be — that has also become our dream.

The right dream — pursued at the right time — infuses our lives with a direction and purpose that gives us the strength and the stamina to achieve it and the inspiration to continue when we feel like giving up. As actor Charles Dutton so eloquently expressed it in the previous chapter, "Having something to believe in is the essence of being on this earth." When we believe in a dream, we are in effect believing in ourselves and our ability to meet our own ideals.

We all know people who have managed to fulfill their dreams early in life. And often we can't help but feel jealous and wonder what it is that they've got that we don't have. When I was struggling to break into broadcast journalism, I sank into a deep depression when I heard that a talented twenty-five-year-old, Jane Pauley — only two years older than I — had been named co-host of "The Today Show." And all I had to show for my job search was a pile of rejection letters. Well, that was eight years ago. Eventually, I did find a good job as a radio reporter and am now working toward a new career as a writer. It may have taken me longer to find my way than the Jane Pauleys of the world, but I can't imagine doing anything else that would have made me happier. The point is that there will always be superachievers who pass us by, and we shouldn't let it bother us. Each of us must move at our own pace, following the internal clocks that set our individual rhythms.

Some of us may make a conscious decision to set the clock back, holding our dreams in abeyance until we feel we are ready, either emotionally or financially, to pursue them or until we can reconcile many conflicting desires. For example, take the case of the father of three who had dreamed of being an artist since early boyhood. As much as he loved painting, he attached equal importance to being a good provider for his family. The art world, of course, is chancy. Most painters, even talented ones, can't rely on receiving a steady paycheck—at least, in the short run. So for two decades he worked in advertising, eventually becoming the head of his own agency. When he felt financially secure, he left advertising to fulfill his lifetime ambition of becoming an artist. For this late bloomer, the postponement of his dream did not mean the abandonment of it altogether. In fact, to a real extent, it facilitated the realization of his dream by permitting him to pursue it free of the financial and emotional burdens that might have forced him to compromise his work at an earlier point in his career.

This path is not peculiar to breadwinners. Their stereotypical counterpart, the breadmakers, follow it as well. Many women put their personal dreams on temporary hold while they fulfill equally compelling family dreams of raising their children and managing their households. Interestingly most of these women do not consider this a hardship or oppressive. On the contrary, they found themselves liberated from the horrible pressure of juggling family, career, children, and personal dreams—in short, the pressure of "having to have it all." When the children were out of diapers and into school, these women focused on themselves and their careers. They discovered, as will we, that it is possible to have it all, as long as we don't have to have it all at once.

As we can see, there are often logical, valid reasons why many of us make a conscious decision to defer our dreams. But there's a big difference between postponing a dream because of conflicting desires and responsibilities and being afraid to pursue a dream because of fear of failure. Some of us are so terrified that we're going to fall flat on our faces, we place roadblocks in our own paths to prevent us from even trying. One way we commit this act of self-sabotage is by setting impossibly high standards for ourselves. We are so determined to be extraordinary that nothing we do is ever good enough . . . so we do nothing.

In her book, *Giving Away Success: Why Women Get Stuck and What to Do About It*, Boston psychologist Susan Schenkel observes that women, who she feels are often overly concerned about what others think of them or their work, often fall prey to this kind of "all or nothing" thinking. "By defining success so narrowly and failure so broadly, we have stacked the odds against ourselves and increased the perceived risks."

Many talented women can identify with this problem, including writer Helen Yglesias, who was fifty-four years old before she finished her first book. Since then her novels, which include *Family Feeling* and *Sweetstir*, have established her as a well-respected author.

Born in 1915 to a traditional Jewish family, Helen became aware of the world during the 1920s, an era of great possibilities. Although her immigrant parents struggled to support their four daughters and two sons, prosperity was in the air. The stock market was booming. America was still the land of opportunity. Women were defying Victorian notions of femininity by bobbing their hair and becoming "career girls." Helen's girlhood dream of becoming an author was fueled by optimism. She was not content to be just any writer; Helen wanted to be a "great" writer producing "great literary works." With unrealistically high expectations, she pursued her goal and, as is often the case, she sabotaged herself in the process.

When Helen was a teenager, she began working on a book based on the experiences of a high-school girl. Disturbed by her preoccupation with what he considered a frivolous pursuit, Helen's dominating, older brother—whom she adored—insisted on reading her manuscript.

Helen recalls the incident in her book *Starting Early, Anew, Over and Late*, which explores the emotional and professional development of herself and others. "I don't remember much of what we said to one another, or if I answered him at all. I remember the word 'perverted.' 'Nobody in the world is going to be interested in that perverted stuff you're writing,' and of course, 'genius'; 'You'd have to be a genius to get away with this boring stuff, and you're no genius.'"

Not satisfied with anything less than "genius," Helen lost her momentum. In tears she shredded her manuscript, page by page. It was much more than a melodramatic gesture by a teenage girl. She had in effect killed her dream in the most insidious way. Never admitting that she had stopped writing, she spent decades starting but never completing her story.

Understanding the circumstances that blocked Helen from

fulfilling her goal sheds some light as to why so many of us who are pursuing lifelong dreams are stopped dead in our tracks.

Helen is the first to admit that some "lousy brother saying, 'Listen kid, you haven't got it'" was not responsible for the four decades of writer's block that followed. Although that incident took its toll, there were many other forces that conspired against her. As she entered early adulthood, the liberated flapper of the 1920s was replaced by a more traditional role model. A woman's career was still considered a transient phase before marriage and motherhood, her *real* vocation. For a woman to succeed in any field, she not only had to be extraordinary but had to *believe* that she was extraordinary. "If someone made it out of the normal women's activities, she was a 'Superwoman,'" Helen said. "She had to be very special. It's one thing to be told that you have to win this race, but it's quite another to be told that you're the *only* woman who can win it."

Another obstacle was Helen's lack of a mentor, either real or imaginary. The well-known women writers whom Helen admired were from privileged backgrounds. Supported by families or husbands, they were freed from the burden of earning a living or raising children, two activities that consumed a great deal of Helen's time. "Virginia Woolf used to talk about being poor, but that was ridiculous. She always had two servants to help her around the house. The same was true of other women writers. They either didn't marry or have children or didn't have to worry about making money."

As if she had been listening to herself and not liking what she heard, she chose her next words with great care. "It was so difficult for women to make it back then. It sounds like I'm making a lot of excuses. 'Oh, this stopped me' or 'Oh, that stopped me.' Yes, they are excuses, but perfectly legitimate ones."

Even when opportunity knocked, Helen was too naive— or too demanding of herself—to answer. In her early twenties, she submitted a short story to *The New Yorker*, which elicited a letter from a top editor offering advice and suggesting revisions. Discouraged, Helen threw the story out, not recognizing the letter as an invitation to try again. If the story wasn't good enough to be published the first time, then it simply wasn't good enough.

Like other members of her generation, Helen was profoundly affected by the Depression. "It made you feel like you were at the bottom of the barrel, especially for young people, people of my age who were just coming out of school. There were no jobs. When you went out looking, you faced a wall of refusal. You brought your expectations down lower and lower. The big thing was to get a job as a salesperson at Macy's."

Abandoning her dreams of independence and a career, Helen married a union official when she was twenty-two. It was considered a good match: her husband was one of the few eligible men around with a full-time job. After the birth of her first child, Helen became a full-time homemaker. When her husband was laid off, she was forced to go back to work. Except for an occasional free-lance editing job that she enjoyed, all she could get were clerical jobs, which she hated.

After World War II, the economy may have made great strides, but the position of women in society took a giant step backward. Freed to work in the offices and the factories during the manpower-hungry days of the war, women were now being sent back to the kitchen and the bedroom. Any woman who was not content to be a wife and mother was, in Helen's words, considered a "psychological misfit."

Helen's marriage fell apart when she fell in love with another man, whom she later married. Ironically her second husband, José Yglesias, was also an aspiring novelist. Unable to earn a living as a writer, José took a job with a pharmaceutical company. Fluent in both Spanish and English, he moved up the corporate ladder with ease, quickly becoming a well-to-do executive. Helen, who by now had three children, stayed at home. She sometimes thought about writing but did very little about it.

Twelve years later, José had his first novel published to excellent reviews. Having saved enough money to support his family for one year, he decided to quit his job to write full-time. To make ends meet, Helen had to get a job.

Like other women who flooded the job market, hoping to reenter the job force, Helen found looking for work in her late forties a humiliating experience. Although she was intelligent and well read, Helen lacked the work experience necessary for anything other than a menial clerical job. Kids fresh out of high school were being paid more than she was being offered. Fortunately she was rescued from her job hunt when the literary editor of *The Nation*, a close family friend, offered her a position as his assistant. Helen thrived at the magazine. She edited manuscripts, proofread galleys, met with writers, and did whatever needed to be done to produce "her" section each month. When her friend and boss died of cancer a year later, Helen inherited his job.

In her early fifties, Helen had come a long way. She had a job that she enjoyed, and although she wasn't writing, she was working closely with other authors. And yet something about her life was incomplete. During a business lunch with British author Christina Stead, whom she deeply respected, Helen mentioned that she had always wanted to be a writer. Stead replied that if she really meant it, she should stop talking about it and start writing. "Just sit down and write the book you mean to write," she instructed Helen. "That's the way it's done. You'll either succeed in handling the material, or you'll fail. If you fail, do it again until you get it right. Of course, there's more to it than that as you know. But the details are nonsense until you sit down to work."

After forty years of excuses and postponements, Helen decided that Stead was right—it was time to "sit down to work." Shortly afterward she quit her job to finish the novel she had begun writing in high school. It would be misleading to suggest that this one incident alone got Helen back on track. Rather it was the culmination of many experiences that led Helen back to her dream. By then Helen had seen enough writers and writing to realize that not everyone produced brilliant work. In fact, she began to see that some of the stories she wrote were just as good as, if not better than, those written by well-known authors. The unobtainably high standards she once had demanded from herself gave way to more realistic expectations.

Helen had developed a new philosophy. "When I was younger, I could only think of great works, great literature. That was the shining reality for me. I finally decided to forget about all that and try to do the best that I can. Let the others decide where it fits into the larger scheme."

Having been married to a writer and working closely with others, Helen knew the mechanics of getting published. She was acquainted with editors, agents, and other people who could open doors. There were also many more women in careers in general and writing in particular—women like her, with husbands and children—whom she could emulate.

In *Starting*, Helen noted that when she began working on her book she felt "a sense of having taken my true life into my hands at long last." As she overcame the obstacles that prevented her from writing, she transformed a pipe dream into a reality.

Pipe Dreams

The difference between a dream and a pipe dream is the act of doing. The pipe dreamer will fantasize. The dreamer will act. Any dream can become a pipe dream if we fail to take the necessary steps to achieve it. This is not to say that the reverse is true—that any dream that doesn't come true was a pipe dream all along. For one thing, some dreams are more difficult to achieve than others, or we might have less control over the outcome. If we dream of becoming a lawyer, for example, chances are that if we get good grades in school, unless some catastrophe strikes, we'll achieve our goal. But if our dreams are more exotic—if we fantasize about becoming the next Bruce Springsteen or Meryl Streep—there's no guarantee that our hard work will ever pay off. Even if we do all the right things—go to acting school, or perform in the hot clubs, or try to meet the right people—we may never make it. The hard truth is that most singers and actors are out of work or working in some other field to support themselves while they look for work as performers. This doesn't mean that we shouldn't try to fulfill our more challenging dreams—as we will see, many late bloomers have beaten the odds and succeeded—only that we may have to work harder and longer to achieve them.

It can take years, sometimes even decades, to accomplish our loftier goals. Very often it is not the most talented or the most beautiful or the best educated who make it to the finish line; it is those of us with the greatest amount of patience and tenacity. For instance, John, a college classmate of mine, dreamed of becoming a network news reporter. After he graduated, John applied to several networks based in New York for an entry-level job. He was turned down by all of them. He was told that the major networks rarely, if ever, hire beginners. The few job openings that crop up in this competitive business are filled by reporters who have been paying their dues at smaller stations throughout the country. Although he didn't want to leave New York, John was determined to get on television So he sent out 150 résumés to TV news directors all over the United States. Within a month he had received two job offers—one in a small town in North Dakota and another in a smaller town in Utah. Because it offered ten dollars more a week than the other job, he accepted the North Dakota job. Before he left for his new home, John admitted that he knew he may never get back to New York as a correspondent, but he strongly believed that the pleasure he would derive from his work would compensate for any reservations he had about leaving the city. A tough reporter and a hard worker, within a year John was hired by a bigger station in the Midwest. A year after that, he became an anchorman in a major market down south. From time to time, John would call to tell me that he still loved his work and that no matter what happened, he was happy with his choice.

John and I fell out of touch, but five years later, when

I was watching a network news show, I was delighted to see that he was back in New York as a correspondent. It took John over a decade, but he had finally "made it" in a highly competitive, difficult field. Although John is not a late bloomer, the example he set is one from which we all can learn. John divided his big dream—being a network correspondent—into smaller, more obtainable goals. Everyday he methodically pursued a tiny piece of his dream until he eventually fulfilled it. But perhaps the most important lesson we can learn from John is that when we strive for a difficult dream, we also have to be prepared to fail. When John left New York, he knew that he might never return. But he found as much satisfaction in the process of achieving his dream as in the realization of the dream itself. It didn't matter to him where he lived as long as he was doing the work that he loved and was making steady progress in his career.

Those of us who are pursuing careers in high-risk, competitive fields must periodically ask ourselves if the struggle is worth it. Every six months or so, we should conduct our own personal audits in which we force ourselves to answer some tough questions. Do we still find our work fulfilling? Are we making slow but steady progress? Or do we feel like we're running in place—exhausted but getting nowhere? And finally, and I believe most importantly, we should ask ourselves if we are still happy with our choice? As we reevaluate our situation, we may decide that we are no longer willing to pay the price of pursuing a dream that is fast becoming a pipe dream. Some of us may look for a new dream, and some of us may decide to redirect the focus of our dream—to keep the essence of the dream but not the dream itself.

That's what entrepreneur Wally Amos did. Better known as "Famous Amos" of chocolate-chip-cookie fame, Wally had to redirect an early dream before he could achieve his extraordinary business success. Ironically Wally opened the first of what was to become a chain of cookie stores in 1975, when, for the first time in his life, he decided that making a lot of money was not that important. "I just wanted to be happy," he recalled. "I never planned on opening more than one store. By then I had lost all desire for material wealth and material success."

Born in 1936, Wally has had a half-dozen different careers, four children, and three marriages. (He is now happily married to artist Christine Harris.) Although his tumultuous life has not been easy, Wally firmly believes that there is no such thing as a bad experience.

"There's something positive in everything that happens," he asserted. "It's only good or bad when you put a label on it. It all depends on how you view life."

Wally's optimistic view of life is a bit mystifying considering that his early years were such difficult ones. Raised in Tallahassee, Florida, until his parents separated when he was twelve, Wally spent the remainder of his youth living with his Aunt Della in New York. Legend has it that one of his happiest childhood memories is eating his Aunt Della's home-baked chocolate chip cookies. Although he was poor, Wally refuses to say anything negative about his childhood. In fact, while some people might lament on how they were forced to shine shoes and deliver newspapers to make money, true to character, Wally turns these menial jobs into early entrepreneurial successes. "I have always been an achiever," he explained proudly. "I've done well in all my jobs, whether I was shining shoes or baking cookies."

At seventeen, Wally dropped out of the New York City Food Trades Vocational High School to join the air force. Stationed in the Deep South, Wally encountered a great deal of racial discrimination. He recalls one incident when he walked out of an airport coffee shop in Mobile, Alabama, because he refused to eat standing up in the back "where the colored people are served." Such occurrences saddened but did not embitter him. "I know there are people who don't like me because of the color of my skin, but I never spent a lot of time thinking about it," he said matter-of-factly.

After his stint in the service, Wally returned to New York and enrolled in a local business school where he became proficient in typing, bookkeeping, shorthand, and other office skills. Upon completing the program, he quickly landed a job as a trainee in the supply department of Saks Fifth Avenue. Within a few months, he married his girlfriend and they soon had a son. Four years and several promotions later, Wally quit his job when his boss refused to give him a five-dollar-a-week raise. Wally soon found that good jobs, especially those that promoted advancement, were scarce. Discouraged, Wally halfheartedly considered applying for a job in the sanitation department or driving a cab. After an intense search, he found the perfect springboard to bigger and better things as a trainee in the music department of the William Morris Agency.

Dubbing himself the "Jackie Robinson of the theatrical agency business," in less than one year Wally became the agency's first black agent. A sharp eye for talent and a natural flare for promotion contributed to his rise in the agency. A desire to strike out on his own spurred him to leave William Morris seven years later to become a personal manager to such celebrities as South African trumpeter Hugh Masakela and actress Pat Finley, who played Bob's sister on "The Bob Newhart Show."

Divorced from his first wife, Wally moved to Los Angeles. He dreamed of launching one of his clients into superstardom and, in the process, becoming one of the town's elite superagents. He was a man consumed by ambition. Although he had remarried, his family took a backseat to his pursuit of wealth and material success. Evenings and weekends were spent at nightclubs, concerts, or recording sessions in search of new clients or to boost the careers of the old.

In his autobiography, *The Face That Launched a Thousand Chips*, he recalled this period with some regret: "My overzealous desire to succeed as an agent led me to neglect other, more personal areas, namely my family." His second marriage eventually ended in divorce.

Wally's career and spirits sank to a low point when he had a falling out with Masakela. At the same time, several other clients began displaying egos that exceeded their earning potential. In debt to the Internal Revenue Service, short of cash, and low on prospects, Wally drastically altered his opulent Beverly Hills life-style to one more compatible with his modest cash flow and moved his office to a less desirable part of town. Tired of struggling and frustrated by his inability to fulfill his dream of becoming a superagent, Wally made a major decision: He would leave show business. "I had been in the business for fourteen years," he explained, "seven years as an agent and seven years as a manager. I finally realized that the big star I was waiting for might never come. Or it could be ten years down the road, and I would have wasted ten years of my life."

During this emotionally charged period while Wally was pondering his future, he turned to an unconventional form of therapy: cooking. Following Aunt Della's recipe and adding some secret ingredients of his own, Wally baked dozens of cookies everyday, giving them away to friends. One day, when he and a friend were munching on a fresh batch, she casually suggested that they open a cookie store.

Wally, who loved the idea, moved on it quickly. Armed with a modest proposal for one store, Wally set out to raise capital for his business venture. After being rejected by local banks and the Small Business Administration, Wally turned to friends for help. Celebrities such as Helen Reddy and her former husband, Jeff Wald, and the late singer Marvin Gaye became investors, while others volunteered advice and other services.

In March 1975, with much publicity and fanfare, Wally opened the country's first chocolate-chip-cookie store in Los Angeles. Wally would have been content to earn a solid, sensible living running one very popular cookie store. His onetime obsession of making it big was no longer as important as feeling good about what he was doing.

Oddly enough, as he began to relax, his cookie empire grew. More and more stores throughout the country began to carry Famous Amos Cookies featuring a photograph of Wally on the package wearing a tattered straw hat and embroidered pullover shirt. Soon Wally was on the cover of *Time* and stories on his phenomenal success appeared in newspapers and magazines all over the world. Without even trying, Wally had finally found his superstar—it was himself.

The irony of his tale is not lost on Wally. "For years, I was trying to make things happen and suddenly, when I stopped trying to control everything, when all I wanted to do was make an excellent chocolate chip cookie and have some fun doing it, my whole life turned around," he mused.

Wally's newfound happiness brought about a spiritual rebirth that he describes in religious terms. "God is in charge," he explained. "I perceive God to be an energy or a spirit that's in the universe that is available to everybody. I didn't create myself; therefore, I can't create anything else. Things are created through me. I'm just a channel through which ideas flow."

Last year Wally, who lives in Hawaii with his wife, Christine, became a father for the fourth time. But for the first time he was present at the birth of his daughter, an experience he found to be a tremendous revelation. "I was able to see that we're all created the same way. From birth, we all have the potential to do anything," he said.

Wally never abandoned his dream; instead he transformed what had become an unobtainable goal—a pipe dream— into a dream that was within his reach. Once he stopped searching for the "superstar," he freed himself from the burden of achieving unrealistically high expectations. The desire to be a well-respected agent is a realistic goal. Wanting to be a *super*-agent—or for that matter, a *super* anything—can have a crippling effect. No matter what you do, it's never good enough.

By redirecting his dream, Wally was able to focus his drive and talent on something that brought him success and peace of mind. I'm not suggesting that by relaxing and reducing the pressure that we place on ourselves, we will all end up as happy multimillionaire entrepreneurs. A success as spectacular as Wally's is rare, and he is a unique and talented person. But from Wally's story, we can see how self-destructive it can be to push ourselves continually to fulfill our big dreams without taking the time to savor our smaller but equally meaningful accomplishments.

Rediscovering an Ideal

Some of us may dream of creating superstars or building corporate empires or even writing the great American novel. These are dreams of personal self-fulfillment. Some of us, however, have more abstract, idealistic dreams that reflect strong personal beliefs. These dreams reflect our vision of the kind of world in which we would like to live.

When John F. Kennedy looked to the one brief shining moment of Camelot as the symbol of his administration and Martin Luther King cried out "I have a dream," both men were revealing their unique and personal vision of the world. Kennedy looked beyond the rough and tumble of back-room politics to the grace and chivalry of a bygone era. King saw past the hatred and bigotry of the real world to a better world where all people are treated equally regardless of their race. These ideals provided both men with a direction and a purpose that shaped their lives.

Idealism, especially in its political context, is often associated with youth. As we get older, we're often forced to make compromises to achieve pragmatic goals that may take precedence over our idealistic dreams. Sometimes we are forced to make agonizing choices. During her first week at a prestigious law firm, my friend Joan, an ardent feminist, was assigned to a sex-discrimination case defending an employer who had fired a woman after he learned that she was pregnant. When Joan explained to a partner that she in good conscience could not accept this case because it violated her beliefs, he replied curtly, "Well, then, perhaps you're in the wrong business," and left the file on her desk.

There may have been times when Joan felt that she was, indeed, in the wrong business, but she handled the case and stayed at the firm. Why? Because most of the time, she enjoyed the work and was extremely well paid for her efforts.

I know several other antiestablishment "New Leftists" of the 1960s who are now happily working for Fortune 500 companies. Have they "sold out"? Perhaps they have in the naive rhetoric of the sixties. But in reality, as we mature and finally see vast expanses of gray where we used to see only black and white, we become less rigid in our beliefs. Also, suddenly overloaded with new responsibilities—supporting ourselves and our families, raising children and building careers—we often make reasoned choices to sacrifice ideals for immediate needs.

We may drift far away from our youthful idealistic dreams and then one day, if circumstances permit, rediscover them and bloom in the process. It can be one of the most rewarding experiences in our lives, as science teacher Marten Tafel learned.

In an era when teachers in general and science teachers in particular are abandoning teaching for more lucrative positions in industry, Marten, of Staples High School in Westport, Connecticut, unabashedly loves his work. So much so, that in 1980, when he reached the state's mandatory retirement age of seventy, with the support of the Westport Board of Education, he fought for the right to continue teaching. It was a rough battle. The ACLU—an organization he had long respected—refused to represent him. He still doesn't understand why. His own teachers' association was lukewarm to the idea. "They said that there wasn't a ground swell of people clamoring not to retire," he explained with a grin. Undaunted by the lack of support, Marten hired a lawyer to sue the State of Connecticut. He won, albeit on a technicality, resulting in the Connecticut legislature's repeal of the law. "I don't mind if the insensitive teachers are fired, but I don't think it's right that someone should be forced out just because of chronological age," he said.

Claiming he will retire only when he feels he is no longer reaching his students, Marten seems to improve with age. In 1984 he was selected by the National Science Teachers Association to receive its Distinguished Service to Science award. "It was a very beautiful thing. It means a lot to me," he said.

A vigorous, gray-haired man with a firm handshake, a quick sense of humor, and an ebullient personality, Marten traces his interest in teaching science back to his youth. As a child, he and his parents, both Russian immigrants, lived in Hell's Kitchen, a rough section of Manhattan. Describing himself as a "healthy, troublesome youngster" who felt pent up in the city, at thirteen, Marten's parents shipped him off to a relative in Stelton, New Jersey, a utopian socialist community founded by former garment industry workers.

He spent the next year and a half in a progressive school named after Francisco Ferrer, a Spanish anarchist and teacher. The school was unique in that it lacked a specific curriculum: Students were encouraged to pursue whatever subjects interested them. It was a sharp contrast to the rigid New York City public school Marten had previously attended where students were forced to sit quietly in rows of identical desks like obedient soldiers.

Stelton was an exhilarating environment that shaped the

course of Marten's life. Away from the concrete of the city, he discovered nature, learning how to hunt, fish, raise chickens, and milk cows. The Ferrer school emphasized hands-on experience over book learning. Students were taught how to read by working at a community newspaper where they not only wrote stories but also set the type and ran the printing press.

Since Stelton did not have a high school, Marten attended a local school where he was shocked by the discipline of the conventional classroom. "I was always full of hell and in trouble with the teachers. I got thrown out of school a few times. The school just didn't allow kids to work off their energies the way kids should."

Fortunately he had an excellent science teacher who encouraged Marten to work on the student-run farm. "I grew acres of potatoes by hand. I cleaned stinking chicken coops in the summertime the old fashioned way, with a shovel. And I loved it," Marten said.

At Rutgers University in New Jersey, Marten studied horticulture. When he graduated from college in 1930—during the height of the Depression—his dream of becoming a landscape architect was shattered when he couldn't find a job in his field.

Marten had no choice but to go to work for a struggling dress-manufacturing company owned by his family. The business had its ups and downs. At a low point all the family had left were two sewing machines, a typewriter, and a safe. Still Marten couldn't complain. The streets were filled with hungry, desperate people lining up outside soup kitchens for a handout. Even if Marten wasn't doing what he wanted—even if the business was rocky—at least he had enough to eat.

Drafted into World War II, Marten was sent to Europe where he met his future wife in Belgium. When they returned to the United States, Marten went back to his old job. The marriage was short-lived. "My wife was still playing the field," Marten joked. In a more serious vein, he explained that his wife had grown up under the Nazi regime in Belgium. "It was a very different morality back then. You did what you had to do to live or else. . . . She was raised under strange conditions."

In 1952 Marten quit the family company when a recession sent shock waves through the garment industry. Marten and his new wife, an antique dealer from Connecticut, left New York to restore an old colonial farmhouse in Wilton. For about five years, the couple ran an antique business that was well regarded among collectors but not very profitable for its owners. When the business began to sour, Marten began investigating other alternatives.

The launching of *Sputnik* by the Soviet Union in the late 1950s changed the direction of Marten's life. In an effort to compete with Russia's technological superiority in space, the United States hastily established programs to train science teachers. Knowing of her husband's interest in botany and his growing frustration with the antique business, Marten's wife suggested that he become a teacher. Close to fifty and out of the classroom for nearly three decades, Marten was apprehensive about making such a major career change. His fears were assuaged after he observed a science class at a local high school. "I felt a tremendous excitement at what I had seen. It wasn't love at first sight, but I knew the potential was there," he said.

In 1959 he completed a master's degree from Yeshiva University in New York and was hired as an intern at a junior high school in Connecticut. After the first difficult year of taming boisterous eighth-graders, Marten found teaching to be the most rewarding work experience of his life. Taking great pride in making science come alive for his students, he emphasized the relevance of what they were learning in the classroom to their daily lives.

"What I find so satisfying about teaching is the look on the students' faces when they finally understand what I'm saying. It's that 'Oh, yeah, that's what he meant' expression when their faces light up. There's nothing that can compare to that experience," he explained.

Marten has very strong opinions on education that he traces back to his year and a half at the progressive school in Stelton. "My whole attitude in the classroom was colored by that experience," he said. "I learned that not all kids are the same. They don't eat the same foods, they don't breathe the same way, they don't have the same interests. It's only logical that you can't teach them all the same way. There's a tendency today to follow a definite curriculum as if you're trying to crank out a bunch of frankfurters. That kind of thinking is wrong."

The same ideals that gave meaning to Marten's life in his early years give meaning to his life today. Had his youth been uninterrupted by the Depression and World War II, he might have fulfilled his need to be near nature by becoming a landscape designer. It seems probable that at some point in his career he would have been attracted to teaching, perhaps by taking on young apprentices or teaching part-time at a high school or college.

Like millions of others, unpredictable events ambushed Marten on the road to achieving his dreams. Although he took a thirty-year detour, he found his way back. The strength of his ideals prevented him from becoming hopelessly lost.

Would the world be a better place if people like Marten Tafel were able to fulfill their dreams "on time"? Not necessarily. All of us have had teachers who after five or ten years in front of a classroom followed the lesson plan word by word as they counted down to retirement. Marten Tafel approaches each class with a sense of wonder and a respect for the individuality of his students. His work is still fresh and exciting, and when it no longer is, he will go on to something else.

Marten describes teaching as "part of the full flow of my life." In mid-life he began his journey back, renewing the values and ideals he cherished as a youth. Completing the cycle, Marten is ready to bloom again. In June 1985 he is planning on retiring from classroom teaching to pursue new dreams. In addition to traveling around the United States, he would like to write a science textbook "that is encouraging rather than intimidating." And Marten—the perennial teacher—would like to organize workshops for other teachers suffering from burnout. "I'd like to help them get excited about their jobs again," he explained.

In an ideal world, we would all be able to fulfill all of our dreams. But since we don't live in a perfect world, some dreams must be postponed—sometimes indefinitely. A homemaker may slow down the progress of her career to raise small children. As the years pass by, she wonders if she'll ever catch up. A father with a family to support who dreams of a career change may not make the move until he is financially stable. Somehow it's never the right time for him to take the plunge. We are constantly reordering our priorities, deferring old dreams to make room for new ones. Some dreams get lost in the shuffle. We may continually put them off until it is no longer possible to achieve them. We lose hope, and then we watch helplessly as they slip away. But if our dreams are strong enough, they don't have to die. Even though they may lay dormant for years on end, the right set of circumstances breathes new life back into them.

A case in point is Olivia Ward, who after thirty-five years as a teacher and principal in New York City public schools retired to pursue a lifelong goal of becoming an actress.

Over the past two years, Olivia has co-starred in a feature film, *Tenement*, and has also appeared in four soap operas, one off-Broadway play and as a bit player in Francis Ford Coppola's *The Cotton Club*. Offstage the attractive fifty-plus mother of two is the wife of New York City's first black police commissioner, Benjamin Ward.

Describing herself as "pleasantly plump," Olivia is continually dieting to shed a once matronly schoolteacher image. Like other aspiring actresses, her days are filled with acting and voice lessons, as well as auditions for parts in commercials and dramatic roles.

"I'm going to get into something big, something good," Olivia predicted confidently. "It's just a matter of when and where."

From an early age, Olivia, who was raised in a suburb of Baltimore, felt that she was destined for the stage. Her mother, a cook for such celebrities as Billy Rose, wanted the best for her daughter. Recognizing Olivia's talent—and believing that it would help develop poise—she paid for her daughter's singing and acting lessons out of her modest wages. When Olivia graduated from high school at the young age of fifteen, she pleaded with her mother to send her to New York to study acting. Horrified at the suggestion, her mother admitted that all her life she had dreamed that her daughter would be a teacher. "Acting is a difficult profession for a white girl, but it's a dead end for a black girl," she told her daughter.

At her mother's insistence, Olivia enrolled in a local teachers' college and graduated at nineteen. She taught school for three years before applying to a master's program at the University of Maryland. Despite her excellent credentials, Olivia was rejected from the then-segregated institution because she was black. Justice—or at least some bizarre form of justice—eventually prevailed. Supreme Court Justice Thurgood Marshall, then the legal counsel for the NAACP, sued the school on behalf of all black applicants. While upholding the school's right to maintain its segregationist policies, a state court ruled that the publicly funded university had an obligation to offer black students an equal education. A compromise was worked out in which the University of Maryland agreed to pay the tuition of black applicants as long as they went to another school. Olivia seized the opportunity to do her graduate work at New York University, just a stone's throw away from Broadway.

"I was thrilled. I was finally getting to New York, and they were paying for everything, my carfare, room, and board," Olivia said.

New York offered Olivia the excitement for which she had been yearning. While working toward her master's in early childhood education, she also studied acting at NYU. In 1950, after she received her degree, she desperately tried to break into the theater, answering casting calls and making the rounds of producers' offices. There were precious few roles for white ingenues, but parts for black actresses were virtually nonexistent. Olivia did get some bit parts in small productions, but the jobs lasted for only a few weeks at a time. The pay was terrible. She remembers the time that she was left with only forty-five cents in her pocket until payday the following week. With sadness Olivia realized that once again she would have to put her dream on hold.

Teaching during the day in a Brooklyn school, Olivia pursued her doctorate in education at night. On her way to work every school morning, she passed a tall, good-looking policeman who patrolled her street. One morning he said hello to her, and she said hello back. A few years later they were married and moved to a suburban Queens community to raise their children.

Ambitious and hardworking, Olivia eventually became district supervisor for early childhood education. Although she never abandoned her dream of becoming an actress, she found that she had a real flair for teaching. "I love children, and I couldn't allow their little minds to be wasted," she said. Olivia, who tried to pass her love of music on to her students, proudly noted that she designed the curriculum for music education that is still being used by the Board of Education. Of course, Olivia leapt at every chance that came her way to sing with church or neighborhood choral groups and to perform in school plays.

Olivia rose in the ranks, finally becoming principal of a public school in Queens. Although she was happy with her accomplishments, the nagging desire to be an actress just wouldn't go away. Knowing of her secret ambition, a friend told Olivia about a local theater group that was in the process of casting an all-black musical. "They're still looking to fill the part of a madam of a speakeasy. You'd be perfect for that," she said mischievously.

At first Olivia dismissed the idea, assuming that she was

too old for the role. Her desire to perform, however, got the better of her. She went to the audition and won the part easily.

It wasn't easy running a school during the day and becoming a musical-comedy star at night. The rigorous rehearsal schedule was exhausting. As tired as she got, and Olivia got very tired, she never before felt as happy or as alive.

After the play finished its short run and the excitement died down, Olivia couldn't bear the thought of returning to the predictable role of an elementary-school principal. Having completed nearly thirty-five years as an educator, she decided it was time to retire. She instinctively realized that she was not the type of person who could waste away her days sleeping late and watching soap operas. Since her husband led an extremely active life, Olivia knew it was critical for her to have something meaningful in her life, or she would feel completely left out.

Between her pension and her husband's income, she was financially comfortable. For the first time in her life, Olivia was free to do whatever she wanted. The answer suddenly seemed obvious—she should pursue the one thing that she really loved: acting. As soon as she left her job, she enrolled in the Lee Strasberg Theatrical Institute. At first Olivia was shy and self-conscious about her age, attending classes with students who were in their early twenties. Olivia's self-confidence grew as her talent and sheer joy for her second career won her the respect of her teachers and fellow students.

At the suggestion of the school, Olivia took additional singing lessons from a well-respected voice coach who works with a number of aspiring and established celebrities. In one of her classes, she caught the eye of fellow student, actress Geraldine Fitzgerald, who, impressed by Olivia, arranged for her to audition for an off-off-Broadway show she was producing, *Take Me Along*. After several callbacks, Olivia was cast as the lead's understudy and had an opportunity to perform several times. Since then, Fitzgerald has become Olivia's mentor, serving as both a guide and a role model. "She's a lovely woman, and she's also been a big help to me," Olivia said.

Olivia was finally channeling her incredible drive and energy into something that she really wanted to do. She began to excel at her new profession, getting small parts at first and then bigger ones in movies and soap operas. Like other actresses, Olivia has had her share of rejections. "It hurt at first, but now I realize that they're not rejecting me as a person but as a type," she said philosophically.

Although Olivia occasionally regrets that she was unable to fulfill her dream earlier in life, she notes that there are real advantages to pursuing acting as a second career. "I don't have to worry about money now. So many of the kids I meet in the business live from paycheck to paycheck. I don't have that problem."

In addition to financial security, Olivia is more secure in terms of her own ability. "I bring to each role a broad range of life experience. I have suffered pain. I'm more sensitive to other people's problems. All these things have made me a better actress." She paused and reflected. "I guess this is the right time for me."

Olivia's dream didn't die because she didn't let it die. Throughout her teaching career, she was "rehearsing" for the next role, performing whenever she had a chance.

Although she couldn't "have it all" at once, she never abandoned her dream and continually found ways to incorporate it into her everyday life. And so can we.

There's an important lesson that we can learn from Olivia and the other late bloomers in this chapter. If we can't fulfill our dreams right away, it doesn't mean that our dreams are doomed. Not at all. If we keep our dreams active by working toward them, step by step, we too could end up being late bloomers.

CHAPTER 4

Mentors and Tormentors

- A college-age daughter arranges for her mother to take the law-school entrance examination. The mother is now a third-year law student.

- The Speaker of the United States House of Representatives gives a new congresswoman choice committee assignments. Eight years later her party nominates her for vice president of the United States.

- A famous actress spots a talented newcomer in her singing class and arranges for her to audition for an off-off-Broadway show. She gets the part, and her acting career is launched.

• The wife of an actor encourages her reluctant husband to run for Governor of California. He follows her advice. Today he is President of the United States.

In each of these cases, one person—either a friend, a relative, or a colleague—played a significant role in guiding and shaping the career of another. Such relationships are not necessarily rare. We all are surrounded by people who can help us bloom and fulfill our dreams. This process is called mentoring. And by understanding these special relationships—and how to make them work for us—we can both give and get more out of life.

It may surprise you that I use the term *mentor* to describe some of the examples listed at the beginning of this chapter. For many of us, the word *mentor* conjures up an image of an older, established person who takes a younger protégé under his or her wing. In the traditional sense, the mentor is guide, role model, and at times "godfather" to his protégé as he climbs the ladder of success. The concept dates back to Homer's *Odyssey*, in which Mentor served as a surrogate father to Telemachus, Ulysses's son. Throughout the ages there have been famous mentor-protégé relationships including that of Leonardo da Vinci and his apprentice Michelangelo and, more recently, that of psychoanalyst Sigmund Freud and his protégé Carl Jung, who eventually parted ways after a serious philosophical disagreement.

In recent years, since psychologists have described the critical roles that they can play in our lives, a great deal of attention has been focused on the role of mentors. In *The Seasons of a Man's Life*, Daniel Levinson describes mentoring in great detail, setting strict sex, age, and time guidelines. According to Dr. Levinson, a mentor is usually male, eight to fifteen years older than his protégé, who is also usually male. When the protégé enters a new stage of development, somewhere in his early thirties, he pulls away from his mentor in the process of "becoming one's own man."

By now those of us other than young men on traditional career tracks should be justifiably concerned. Women might question the male orientation of Dr. Levinson's description. "His" protégé? One's own "man"? What about us—do we miss out on this important relationship? Late bloomers might ask, "What about people like me who stray from traditional timetables? Am I too old to have a mentor even though I may need one?"

Fear not. There's no reason why any of us must struggle through life without the comfort and support of a mentor. It is true, however, that most of us may not have the *traditional* mentor-protégé relationship. Instead many will experience what I call "limited mentorships," which I describe later in this chapter.

In terms of traditional mentor-protégé relationships, Dr. Levinson is correct in his observation that mentor is often synonymous with male. The lack of women in high-powered positions creates a shortage of successful older women to mentor younger ones. As any young woman doctor, lawyer, or management trainee knows, finding sympathetic and friendly women role models is extremely difficult if not impossible. To compound the problem, many men are reluctant to mentor women because of sexism or fears that the relationship may be misinterpreted by colleagues.

Just as some mentors shy away from women protégés, some mentors are wary of taking on older protégés. They may seek out someone who is younger, whom they feel they can dominate, or they may feel uncomfortable playing a superior role with someone close in age or older than themselves. And sometimes we ourselves are not receptive to overtures made by prospective mentors. There comes a time in all our lives when we become weary of the role of the impressionable neophyte and need to feel that our judgment is as good as anybody else's.

Nevertheless those of us who are unable or unwilling to take advantage of traditional mentoring relationships need not be left out in the cold. We form our own unique support system—I call them "limited mentorships"—in which the mentor performs a very specific role in the blooming process.

In the broadest definition of the word, there are many different types of mentors. If you think about it, you may have had a mentor and not even known it at the time. For example, perhaps there was someone who was extremely influential in your life—a friend, a relative, or a colleague—who could have served a mentorlike function. Or perhaps you may have emulated a role model who became a kind of mentor.

For late bloomers mentors may serve as catalysts in the blooming process, helping us identify and/or fulfill our life goals. In this capacity a mentor may perform one or more of the following functions.

Shows the way:	In these cases mentors provide specific guidance in a career setting. They show us how to function as professionals. The mentor fills the gap in our education or training, thus providing the finishing touches in blooming.

Hears the "unspoken voices":	These mentors help us identify our dreams. It's a crucial function, since very often we may know that we want to do *something* with our lives but we don't know exactly *what*.
Serves as a facilitator:	The mentor serves as a catalyst to spur us into action.
Serves as an image enhancer:	Sometimes we lack the confidence needed to pursue a dream. Enhancers build up a late bloomer's self-confidence until he or she is ripe for blooming.

Just as mentors perform different functions in our lives, there are several different types of mentors. There are traditional style *career mentors*, older, more experienced people who offer a helping hand in a professional environment. *Professional mentors* are career counselors, psychologists, and other people we hire to help us bloom.

Some of us have mentors that exist only in our minds—*imaginary mentors*, or idols—in which we emulate people whom we revere, although we may never have met them. For example, a whole generation of young writers used Ernest Hemingway as a mentor, studying and imitating his unique style. A relationship to an imaginary mentor is the theme of Woody Allen's film *Play It Again, Sam*, in which the protagonist idealizes a character from another movie— Humphrey Bogart's role in *Casablanca*.

Peer mentors are friends or colleagues with whom we develop supportive mentor-type relationships. *Romantic mentors* are spouses or lovers who serve as "enhancers," giving us the confidence to bloom. I'm not talking about the stereotypical, male-dominated "Svengali"-type relationships in which a strong man masterminds his "weaker" wife's career. These romantic mentorships are equal, two-way, and mutually beneficial unions. At times our family members can serve as mentors in that we can help each other fulfill our goals.

Mother-Daughter Mentoring

We tend to think of our relationship with our parents as being one-sided—we take and they give. Certainly this is true when we're very young and are entirely dependent on them for our survival. But as we get older and attain maturity and gain experience, the scales even out and will often begin to tip in the other direction.

Recent studies confirm that adult children can be a source of great emotional support to their parents. Pennsylvania State University Professor Gunhild Hagestad notes that adult children's growing independence gives parents a "new set of resource persons, namely, young adult offspring." Her findings revealed that mothers tend to turn to their children for guidance and support more often than fathers do, which she attributes to the fact that women tend to be closer to their children during their early years. She concludes that for both men and women "young adult children serve as bridges to the wider social context, mediating cultural and social changes."

This is probably true for every generation, but it is especially true for women who came of age before the rise of the women's movement. These "transitional" women who married in the 1950s and early 1960s suddenly found that by the end of the sixties their world had been turned upside down. The sexual revolution had radically changed sexual mores. Couples were not only engaging in premarital sex but openly living together out of wedlock. Divorce became rampant. And at a dinner party, you dare not confess that you were "just a housewife," because able-bodied women like yourself were now expected to have careers and families. In these confusing times, many parents, especially mothers, began to look to their grown children for advice and support. Mothers watch with admiration as their daughters pursue careers side by side with men in courtrooms, hospitals, and accounting firms. Homemakers who wouldn't dream of asking their husbands for help around the house marvel at their daughters' egalitarian marriages. Slowly, sometimes with much coaxing from their children, these women begin to see that this new world isn't just for their daughters, that it is also for them.

Children who encourage their parents to return to school, seek a job, switch careers, or explore unknown terrain are serving a "limited mentorship" function. Sometimes daughters are trailblazers who "show the way" to their mothers. Often daughters function as "enhancers," assuring their mothers that they *can* do something, as well as offering emotional support.

If done in a heavy-handed way, mentoring by children can seem more like bullying. A few years ago I was the uncomfortable observer of a fight between my neighbor Debby and her mother, Rose. Debby, who believed that she was doing the right thing, kept badgering Rose to "stop wasting her life as a housekeeper" and get a real job. Her mother started crying and saying things such as, "So that's what you think I am—a cleaning woman?" What should have been an open, honest discussion about Rose's desires and needs deteriorated into a shouting match that resulted in much ill feeling.

Mothers don't like to be told what to do by their offspring anymore than their children like being told what to do by them. But if done in a loving, supportive way, we can be sources of help and inspiration to each other. This in no way diminishes a mother's role as a parent. In a good relationship, daughters will continue to seek advice and support from their mothers on everything from child rearing to in-law management. But the best relationships are not one-way. As daughters explore the world on their own, they develop their own insights and methods of coping that they can share with their mothers. Both partners are enhanced by the strengths and experiences of the other.

A case in point is Betsey Nathan, who at forty-seven is now a third-year evening student at Brooklyn Law School, thanks in part to the encouragement of her twin daughters, Ann and Emily, who are also law students. Ann is a second-year student at Brooklyn, while Emily is finishing her last year at NYU.

Unlike many women of her generation, Betsey was raised to have a career. Her mother, a college-educated woman frustrated because she had never worked outside the home, taught her daughter at an early age that a woman must have something of her own outside her marriage. Raised in an affluent Long Island community, Betsey, the daughter of a dentist, knew that she would go to a good college. Nevertheless, she was steered to fairly conventional female occupations. When she once mentioned that she might like to be a lawyer, her mother dismissed the pursuit of law as "too dry." When Betsey later expressed interest in being a doctor to an uncle in medical school, he promptly told her horror stories about the way female students were treated by their classmates and teachers. "There was this one woman who found sugar in a urine sample that they were testing in class. From that point on, she was called Sweet Pee. It sounded just horrible," Betsey recalled with a laugh.

In high school Betsey decided to be a social worker, an occupation that not only fulfilled her desire to help people but was also considered an acceptable one for a woman.

After her sophomore year at Vassar, Betsey married a Johns Hopkins medical student and transferred to nearby Goucher College to finish her degree. By that time her Vassar class had dwindled to half its original size, as women left, as the old joke goes, to get their "MRS."

Since her husband, who worked around the clock, spent little time at home, Betsey fully intended to pursue her graduate degree in social work right after college. After she became pregnant, she postponed her schooling until her daughters were a year and a half old. Managing to juggle caring for two small children with her schoolwork, Betsey received her master's degree in social work in 1963.

From early on in her marriage, Betsey had her doubts about the relationship. Her husband, a dedicated and well-respected physician, was very much concerned with pursuing his career. Any aspirations that she may have had were secondary to his. Although Betsey often felt neglected, she believed that his work, which helped "mankind," was much more important than her feelings of loneliness. From a practical point of view, even if she wanted to leave the marriage, she had no place to go. "At that time there was very little money, so I would have been completely on my own. Also I really didn't feel that I had a lot of choices. I thought that women with children weren't very salable in terms of marriage. So I was stuck," she explained.

In the early 1960s, Betsey remembers being profoundly affected by a controversial new book, *The Feminine Mystique*. Although the rise of feminism would not occur for another decade, Betsey immediately realized that Betty Friedan's prophesies would have a major impact on her daughters' lives. "But I thought it was too late for me," she said.

Working part-time as a social worker, Betsey was the model suburban mother, dividing her time between her job, the P.T.A., and chauffeuring her kids to their various activities.

In 1974 Betsey and her children accompanied her husband on a six-month sabbatical to London, forcing her to quit her job. Alone in a strange country while her husband pursued his professional activities and her kids were in school, Betsey had a lot of time to think. It was the first time that her children no longer required her constant attention. Without a job outside the home to distract her, she felt a great emptiness in her life. As she looked ahead to the future, she didn't like what she saw.

By now in her late thirties, Betsey began to question the premise of her marriage. Were her husband's aspirations and desires really more important than her own? Granted, he was helping "humanity," but wasn't she part of "humanity" too? Should her needs always be subordinate to his career . . . and to "humanity"?

Divorce no longer seemed impossible. The women's movement was in full swing. Wives everywhere were renegotiating the terms of old marriages or leaving unsatisfactory relationships to start new lives. Betsey realized that this new world was not just for her daughters, it was also for her.

When the family returned to the United States, Betsey received a blow: Her part-time job had been filled during her absence. Their mother's predicament made a deep impression on the girls, now fifteen. Emily recalled, "I always thought that mom was extremely competent. It seemed rotten to me that she had to give up her job when we went to England and then not have anything to come back to."

For Ann the entire experience was very disconcerting. "It made me realize for the first time how undervalued our mother was. She was so bright—it just seemed so unfair," she explained.

It came as no surprise to her daughters when Betsey decided that she could no longer stay in a marriage that had ended a long time ago. Although they were still in high school, Ann and Emily were both active in feminist causes. Since they would not be happy in a marriage like their mother's, they did not expect her to be either. In fact, Betsey feels that they might not be as close as they are now had she decided to remain with their father. "They understood why we got divorced. I don't think they would have understood it if I had stayed married knowing how I felt."

After she separated from her husband, Betsey was out of work a few months before landing a job as a social worker. Although her starting salary was low, the money came in very handy since Betsey was now expected to contribute to the support of her family. Shortly after her divorce, friends introduced Betsey to a psychotherapist. They began dating and were married a year later. The unspoken contract in her second marriage was radically different from her first. Betsey entered the marriage on equal footing; her needs were as important as her husband's. "In my first marriage the focus was on promoting my husband's success. This time the focus is on *us*," she explained.

Thriving in this supportive atmosphere, Betsey progressed quickly in her career, rising from caseworker to supervisor to program director. Although she was doing well, Betsey was rapidly reaching the point when after studying or practicing social work for nearly two decades, she was ready for a change. She asked herself, "What do I really want to do with my life?" But she didn't come up with any answers.

Betsey considered leaving the nonprofit world to work for a corporation. Somehow her heart wasn't in it, and she never pursued any leads. Deeply committed to social change, Betsey also toyed with the idea of becoming a public-interest lawyer. She changed her mind after quickly reviewing an old copy of the law-school entrance exam and being intimidated by the math questions.

While Betsey was pondering her future, Emily had hers all worked out, or so she thought. Graduating from Princeton with a degree in history, she planned on spending a year in Manhattan working before pursuing a Ph.D. Emily's plan fell through. She couldn't get a job until late in the summer, forcing her to move back home with her mother. Unhappy that she was still financially dependent on her parents, Emily reached the disturbing conclusion that a background in history was never going to be marketable.

Learning from her mother's experience, Emily realized that a woman can't depend on anyone else to support her; she needed to find a well-paying career. Since she had always been interested in current affairs and politics, she decided to become a lawyer. Emily called the Educational Testing Service in New Jersey to get information on the law boards. She asked the clerk to mail out two applications: one for her and one for her mother.

"I didn't want to take the test alone, and I figured that if we did it together, it wouldn't be so bad," Emily recalled.

At first Betsey resisted the idea. There were still too many math questions and funny-looking graphs—she'd never get past the first page. After being persuaded by Emily to take a closer look at a sample test, Betsey saw that math comprised only a small part of the exam. The rest of the questions dealt with subjects that genuinely interested her. She reasoned that what she didn't know, she could learn at a review course. Betsey and Emily threw themselves into studying for the law boards, meeting every evening to provide each other with help and support.

Three months later they both had been accepted to law school. Ann, who shared her family's concern for social justice and interest in politics, joined her mother the following year at Brooklyn Law School.

While Betsey was deciding what to do with her life, Emily, hearing the "unspoken voices" from within, convinced her mother to do what she really wanted. Would Betsy have eventually found her way to law school without the intervention of her daughter? Maybe. There's no doubt, though, that Emily speeded up the process by urging her mother to take the first step.

Both Emily and Betsey agree that there was something very special about taking the law boards together. It gave them a sense of support and empowerment that they would not have experienced alone. While women often may miss out on traditional mentoring relationships, this unique mother-daughter relationship can help both generations fulfill their goals.

Romantic Mentors

In addition to having daughters who helped "show the way," finding a husband who was more compatible with her goals made a tremendous difference in Betsey Nathan's life. Beyond playing a generally supportive, loving role, our spouses or lovers can also be mentors. In fact, many partners serve as each other's mentors, providing friendship, advice, and guidance as it is needed.

A case in point is former President Jimmy Carter and his wife, Rosalynn. In her autobiography, *First Lady from Plains*, Rosalynn describes how through Jimmy's help and encouragement, she was transformed from a shy, introverted Plains, Georgia, homemaker into a leading member of their community. Through the years, as Jimmy pursued his political career, Rosalynn became more and more involved in his campaigns, often delivering speeches in his place and serving as his personal emissary. In the White House, Rosalynn, an extremely active and independent First Lady, sat in on cabinet meetings, offering her husband advice when he sought it. In one way Jimmy served as Rosalynn's mentor, spurring her on to develop and grow. But in time, as Rosalynn became more experienced and sophisticated, Jimmy turned to her for support and assistance. In the best sense they are each other's mentors, as we are often mentors to our spouses and lovers.

The political arena is filled with examples of mentor

couples. For example, Nancy Reagan has been credited with helping to shape both her husband's political philosophy and his career. In fact, in a recent interview, longtime Reagan associate Lyn Nofziger claimed that Nancy pushed a reluctant Ronald Reagan to run for Governor of California in 1965. Like the Carters, the Reagans are also known for their close relationship and for the wife's role as her husband's adviser and best friend.

All of us can benefit from someone in our lives who makes us feel that we are capable of doing whatever we want. If we're lucky, we get that kind of support early in life from parents and teachers. If we're not, we may have to look elsewhere. Although romantic mentors can serve many functions, they often play the role of image enhancer, making us aware of our potential.

Laurie Sanders* may never have fulfilled a lifetime dream of becoming a writer without a romantic mentor who made her believe that it was possible.

In the quiet, midwestern town where Laurie Sanders grew up, high-school girls from blue-collar families were tracked into typing and steno classes so they could eventually become secretaries. Then they were expected to marry young and have children. Lots of them. Their fate was sealed by the time they were eighteen years old.

Laurie, however, was determined to break the mold. Not only would she go to a good college, but she would become a writer, her ticket to an exciting, creative world that she longed to explore.

Her dream provided refuge from her grim surroundings. An awkward, shy child, Laurie fell prey to her stepfather's cruel teasing and at times physical abuse. "I was never good enough," she recalled bitterly. "All he ever wanted was a cute, blue-eyed blond little girl. I was a sallow, rather homely child."

To escape the painful reality, Laurie withdrew into a fantasy world where she spent her days listening to classical music and reading novels. She didn't care that the other kids were enthralled by Elvis Presley or that they thought her love for Eugene O'Neill's plays was a bit odd. Even if she didn't conform to the norms in her hometown, she would find her niche in college.

In her senior year of high school, Laurie was summoned for the usual talk with the school guidance counselor. In one sentence he shattered all of her dreams. Holding back her tears, Laurie listened quietly as she was told that girls "like her" did not go to college. And they certainly did not become writers. He also pointed out a grim fact that Laurie had conveniently ignored: Her parents couldn't afford to pay her tuition. Even if she was accepted into a college, she could never go. Laurie was devastated. Yet, without money and unaware that things such as scholarships or school loans even existed, she had no choice.

Graduating from high school in 1957, Laurie took a clerical job at a credit bureau for $175 a month. While working as a volunteer in a psychiatric hospital, she met Bill, a recreational therapist and a self-styled beatnik who wrote poetry. Laurie fell head over heels in love with him. Within a few months they were married. Through Bill Laurie encountered a whole new crowd of well-educated but broke Bohemians who always seemed to visit around dinnertime. Never quite included as an equal, Laurie cooked, served, and washed dishes as they discussed art and world events.

At twenty-five Laurie gave birth to her daughter, Jenny. For the first time in a long while, she felt a strong need to put her feelings down on paper. The entry in her diary read, "Why is it I have a wonderful husband, a perfect baby, and yet, I feel so incomplete. Something is missing."

Two more children—a son and a daughter—did not fill the void. Although Laurie loved being a mother, her old dreams began to surface. Extremely frustrated by the fact that she had not become a writer, Laurie wondered if she would ever find fulfillment.

As Laurie's blind love for her husband gave way to a more realistic view, she began to see that the dark moods she had once attributed to the soul of an artist were actually symptoms of severe depression. There were times when Bill was so low, he could not provide her with either the emotional support she craved or the financial support she needed to pay the bills. For comfort and companionship, she turned to an older family friend, Richard, a frequent guest in her home. Also unhappily married, one night Richard confessed that he had had a crush on Laurie that dated back to the first day they met. Shortly afterward they became lovers.

Laurie's relationship with Richard was much more than just an extramarital tryst; it was the major turning point of her life. "For the first time, there was someone who was one hundred percent on my side. He told me I was beautiful. He was the first person who ever told me that I could do anything I wanted—even be a writer," Laurie explained.

There were many evenings when Richard, Bill, and Laurie would sit around her living room and talk. Although Bill and Laurie never discussed her affair, she is certain that he knew about it. "By that time, it didn't matter. We were really just good friends who were living together," she said.

Through her relationship with Richard, Laurie gained a tremendous amount of confidence. She once again began to believe that life was full of possibilities. For example, when Bill was out of work and Laurie needed to get a job, Richard urged her to apply to a small suburban newspaper that had an opening for a part-time reporter. At first she dismissed the idea. After all, she had no experience, she lacked a college degree, and the only writing she had done in recent years was in her diary. Richard kept pushing her until she agreed at least to call for an appointment with the editor. Impressed by her enthusiasm, the editor hired her on the spot. Laurie was thrilled until she heard the salary, sixty-five dollars a week, barely enough to cover the cost of child care. Viewing it as an opportunity to prove herself as a writer, she accepted the offer, even though it meant taking a second job to augment her meager income.

With great gusto Laurie covered the dullest town meetings, wrote feature stories on community fish fries, and even created her own column, a loose mixture of recipes and philosophy. Impressed by her work, the publisher made her editor of a bigger newspaper in the chain.

Eager to sharpen her skills, Laurie enrolled in a journalism workshop at a local college taught by seasoned reporters. The forty-five-minute weekly classes were a revelation to Laurie. Although she had instinctively known the elements of good writing, she had never been formally taught the technique of newspaper reporting. With each new story she wrote, her work improved. As she gained confidence in her ability, she began to develop a unique, folksy writing style that appealed to her suburban readers.

When Laurie learned that a major, prestigious daily newspaper needed free-lance reporters to beef up their suburban section, she immediately called for an appointment to meet with the managing editor. Armed with a portfolio filled with clips, she proudly marched into the impressive city room, ecstatic that she finally had a shot at the "big time."

The editor carefully examined her clips nodding approvingly when he read something he liked. Then he glanced at her résumé, shook his head, and said, "I'm sorry, but we don't hire writers without a college degree. Some of our old-timers don't have degrees, but we're trying to upgrade the educational level of our staff."

For a second Laurie felt as if she was back in high school talking with her guidance counselor. "Girls like you don't go to college." "Girls like you don't become writers."

This time Laurie refused to sit quietly. She was getting very angry. Granted, she didn't have the good fortune to have gone to an Ivy League school. But she had worked very hard to get where she was. She was good and she knew it. And she was going to let this Goddamned editor know it too.

'Well, that's your loss," she replied, not quite believing that the words were hers.

"Oh, is it really? And why is that?" demanded the editor.

"Your west county coverage is weak. I've lived and worked there, and I think you could use my help," Laurie retorted.

"Good-bye," he said as he quickly dismissed her from his office.

Laurie could barely escape from the building before she started to cry. It was her big chance and she blew it. "I was thirty-two years old. I figured that was it, I'd never succeed."

At 10:00 A.M. the next morning, Laurie, still feeling depressed, went to answer the telephone. The suburban editor was at the other end of the line. "Laurie? The boss says he likes your style. How would you like to cover a meeting for us tonight?"

From that point on, Laurie became a frequent contributor to the paper. As her reputation grew, she began to receive a number of other writing assignments from different newspapers and magazines.

When after a long illness, Richard died of a heart attack, Laurie was saddened but not shattered by the loss of her friend. His legacy—the confidence he gave her—lives on. It has helped Laurie improve her life both personally and professionally. After divorcing her husband, she began dating a reporter at the newspaper. They are now happily married.

Of course, it took more than confidence for Laurie to become a well-respected writer. By attending the journalism workshop, she developed the necessary skills to achieve her goal. The reporters who taught the class were limited mentors in that they "showed the way" to aspiring journalists.

Laurie's story is far from over. Finally fulfilling her lifetime dream, she is attending college at night. "A college girl at last," she said with a big smile. "I want to learn everything."

Not Really Showing the Way

Why do so many of us end up in careers that we hate? Sometimes we are victims of bad mentoring. We are sent on wild-goose chases down the wrong path by well-meaning people. Take the case of John Murphy,* an accountant in St. Louis who confessed that he had spent "twenty miserable years" before leaving his accounting practice to open his own restaurant. Why did he become an accountant? "My high-school guidance counselor saw that I had good grades in math and told me that I could make a good living as an accountant," John explained. Not having any goals of his own, he followed her advice. In retrospect he noted one interesting fact: He and the counselor never discussed what being an accountant entailed or whether or not he might like it.

I'm not saying that all high-school guidance counselors are bad. And even if they offer the wrong advice, no one's forcing us to follow it. Unlike John, we must assume responsibility for our own lives. Before we pursue a career at the suggestion of someone else, we should try to investigate thoroughly what that career is like and where it will take us. We should also be wary of the quick, seat-of-the-pants career counseling often offered by well-meaning teachers, friends, parents, and at times professionals that can be extremely damaging.

Bad mentors may honestly believe that they have your best interest at heart. For example, New York psychologist Dr. Loretta Walder observes that many of us go into our "family businesses" without even knowing it. "So many kids get pegged and pushed. They're influenced into doing something that they don't really want to do. They think it's their dream until they wake up," Dr. Walder said.

Sometimes a good mentor knows what a protégé wants even before the protégé knows. Theodore Reik, a renowned psychoanalyst, noted that people in his profession must listen "with a third ear" to the unspoken voices. What Reik meant was that if you work with people, you must have a sixth sense that helps you understand the hidden needs of others. But bad mentors listen with one ear to their own

103

voice. They can't help us fulfill our dreams because they don't know what they are.

There is an enormous difference between good mentoring and bad mentoring. A good mentor is similar to a professional baseball coach who knows how to motivate his players. Sports psychologist Dr. William Beausay of the Academy of Sports Psychology International in Columbus, Ohio, said that a good coach never tells a seasoned player how to swing a bat. "What he does is find out what it takes to get this person, this magnificent piece of machinery, to operate or perform at his optimum level. He asks himself, how does he function best and how can I help him achieve the goals he has set for himself?"

Like the good coach, the good mentor gets his protégé to believe in himself and then lets him carry the ball from there. We should feel appreciative of the help we are getting, not resentful that we are being told what to do. If the relationship begins to feel overbearing, it is time for us to reevaluate the role the mentor is playing in our lives. A *good* mentor, at the right time, can mean the difference between success and failure. Talent, skill, and enthusiasm can only take us so far. Sometimes we need someone to "show the way" before we can become professionals.

In his midtwenties Mark Rossi* made a decision that money was not enough: He wanted a job that offered both psychic as well as financial income. In his quest for self-fulfillment, Mark abandoned a safe, secure career as a dentist for the chancy, competitive world of a professional photographer. Talented, enthusiastic, and ambitious, Mark tried to break into the New York photography scene only to fall flat on his face. At one of the lowest points in his life—

when he was seriously considering abandoning his dream—
Mark found a mentor who showed him how to earn a living
while doing the work that he loved.

Mark's desire for self-fulfillment is a radical departure
from the way he was brought up. Raised in a close, lower-
middle-class Italian family, Mark was taught the virtues of
the "work ethic" at an early age. The Rossis dreamed that
Mark and his older brother would go to college so that they
could eventually pursue steady, respectable careers. "My
parents would have been happy to see me become a teacher
or a manager of a store. I didn't have to like what I was
doing. They felt that I should want what they wanted, which
was to make a good living to support a family."

Although Mark secretly wanted to be an actor, he became
the perfect "all-American kid." "I was a goody two shoes,"
he said with a grin. "When everybody else had long hair,
I had a crew cut. I was president of the student council. I
won letters on the swimming team. I was in the drama club,
good at school," he paused for emphasis. "I was the perfect
little son."

In 1971, when other college freshmen were burning their
draft cards and fleeing to Canada, after drawing a low number in the draft lottery, Mark obediently enlisted in the air
force. "I didn't want to go either," he said. "I was scared.
I'm not a soldier type, but there was no doubt that I was
going. Protesting was not part of my upbringing."

As an assistant to a colonel in the dental corps, Mark
enrolled in a special dental-training program. "I figured that
dentistry was as good a profession as anything else," he
explained with a shrug. Although he wasn't too interested
in the work, he did enjoy his frequent travel assignments,

which included Europe and Asia. On one of these trips he met and fell in love with an army nurse, whom he later married.

"I wasn't a strong person back then," Mark recalled. "I did everything everybody told me to do. Society says that you register for the draft, you go to college, you get married, do your time in the service, and then get a job when you get out. I was just following the formula."

Over the next two years, Mark's view of the world began to change. Frequent separations as a result of conflicting schedules placed enormous pressures on his marriage. As he and his wife drifted apart, Mark began to contemplate the possibility of divorce. The painful realization that following the "formula" doesn't always guarantee a happy ending had a domino effect on Mark, as he began to reexamine other aspects of his life.

Away from home and his family's influence, Mark was exposed to many different cultures and life-styles. He observed that people who seemed to lead the fullest lives were those who were pursuing professions that they enjoyed. It suddenly dawned on him that he had never really thought about work in terms of what he wanted to do. Work equaled money and nothing more. And yet something deep inside him rebelled against the thought of spending his life doing something that he didn't find fulfilling. During an intense period of self-examination, Mark reached a startling conclusion: After three and a half years of dental school, he finally realized that he hated the thought of being a dentist. "I didn't like anything about it," he said with a grimace. "Sticking my fingers in dirty mouths was not fun. It's a thankless job. A dentist sees nothing but problems all day. I'm not the kind of person who wants that."

Mark's announcement that he was leaving the military and dropping out of dental school elicited a sharp reaction from family and friends. During long and painful telephone conversations, Mark held his ground as his mother pleaded with him to reconsider and his father kept saying sadly, "I don't know why you're doing this." Finally his parents reconciled themselves to their son's decision. Both in tears, they told Mark, "We may not agree with you or understand what you're doing, but we love you anyway."

Emotional support from an older brother, John, who had always been the rebel of the family, helped him through this extremely difficult period. "He was the first person in my family who ever told me that I was the only one who had to answer for my life. He urged me to do what I wanted to do, not what I thought was expected of me. He may have only said it a couple of times, but he helped me to come to terms with myself," Mark said.

Hoping to find direction, Mark looked for examples of "happily successful" people whom he could emulate. Sol, a close family friend who owned a photography lab, was someone who fit the bill—he did extremely well at something that he truly enjoyed. So when Mark heard that Sol was looking to hire a part-time assistant, he jumped at the chance to work with him. After Mark demonstrated a real aptitude for the job, Sol casually suggested that he take a few courses at a professional photography school.

From the first week of classes, Mark knew that he was in the right place, having finally found something that not only captivated his interest but also enabled him to use his creativity. "All the pieces suddenly came together," he said. "I was able to use my artistic ability in a career that would also provide me with a secure job. I am still very much my parents' son, and it is very important for me to have a steady job that people respect."

After graduating from school in 1978, determined to conquer the world of photography, Mark quickly saw that competition was fierce. Establishing himself in New York was not going to be easy. There were many good photographers pounding the pavement with portfolios in hand, trying to make a name for themselves. Not to mention the fact that a handful of well-known studios got the lion's share of assignments. As he tried to build a business, he took on odd jobs to earn a living. In 1980, broke and frustrated, he was considering making yet another career change when he cut his thumb on a slicing machine while waiting tables in a restaurant. Unable to work for three weeks while his thumb healed—and in desperate need of a change of scenery— Mark decided to visit Rick, an old army friend in Atlanta.

Georgia provided Mark with a welcome respite from the New York rat race. One night, while telling Rick about his faltering career, his friend suggested that Mark apply for a job at a famous Atlanta photography studio. Mark bristled at the notion of quitting his hometown but agreed at least to give the studio a call. He managed to speak with Jeremy Schoen, a well-known local photographer who told Mark that he'd be delighted to look over his work, but that there were absolutely no job openings. Mark made the date anyway. Mark and Schoen hit it off immediately. "There was an electricity between us, the excitement that we both shared about our general concepts in life, our feelings about photography. Everything was right," Mark recalled. By the end of the discussion, Schoen had offered Mark a job, which he immediately accepted.

When Mark joined the studio, he had the talent if not

the experience to be a first-rate photographer. From Schoen he learned how to earn a living while doing the work he loved. Schoen provided the model Mark needed to become a professional. "I learned all the things you need to know and don't learn in a classroom," he observed. "In New York a lot of photographers are so busy trying to be artists, that they forget that you're also supposed to make a living from your work." For the first time in his life, Mark had a paycheck and a job he enjoyed. Yet Mark still "wanted more." The kind of exciting assignments he yearned for could only be found in New York. He was torn between fulfilling his dream or staying in a steady-paying job. The prospect of starting over in New York was a frightening one. It took Mark more than a year to summon up the courage to move back. "I knew I was procrastinating. I finally said, 'I've got to do it or forget about it.'"

At age thirty, Mark left Atlanta to open up his own studio in Manhattan. The first few months in his new business were rough, but Mark felt equal to the challenge. "Just by beginning to do it, I saw that I was really ready. I definitely knew that this time I was going to be successful." And he was.

Mark landed several plum photography assignments, including a Christmas catalog for a major New York City department store. He is doing so well, in fact, that he recently hired a young photographer fresh out of school to work as his assistant. "He reminds me of me," Mark explained. "He's young and eager to start his own studio. I'm trying to teach him how to do it. I guess I'm doing for him what Jeremy did for me."

Successful people seem to have a knack for finding mentors at just the right time, and Mark is no exception. When he needed emotional support, he found a friend in an older brother. When he needed career guidance, he found a teacher who directed him to professional school. And when he needed someone to show him the tools of the trade, he found Jeremy Schoen who altered the outcome of Mark's life. And now, Mark, an established photographer, is no longer in need of a mentor—he is a mentor.

Throughout our lives we are surrounded by people who can help us develop and grow and fulfill our dreams. It is our responsibility to find these people and to seek guidance when we need it. Of course, we can't rely on another person to show us how to live our lives—that we have to figure out for ourselves. But as we search for direction, we can look to others for emotional support and practical advice. Being a protégé is not a passive role. We also have a job— to take the best of what our mentors have to offer and to incorporate it into our lives. When we reach a point at which we no longer need a mentor, we should plant some seeds of our own and, like Mark, find someone else whom we can help bring to bloom.

CHAPTER 5

Till Change Do Us Part

*I*magine *that you're lying in bed, and your* husband, wife, or lover turns to you and says, "I'm ready for a change in my life." Your mouth goes dry. Your palms get sweaty. Your stomach starts doing cartwheels as you focus on that dreaded word *change*.

Panicky thoughts race through your head. What does she mean by change? Why is he unhappy? What am I doing wrong? How is all of this going to affect me?

For most of us, the prospect of any kind of change—a new job, moving to a strange neighborhood, or beginning a new relationship—can be frightening. Change means leaving the comfort of the familiar for the terrors of the

111

unknown. We are scared of the imaginary demons that lie waiting in ambush down every twist and turn of our life's path.

The prospect of a major change in our marriage or partnership is the most difficult of all with which we must cope. Marriage is our sanctuary, an anchor of safety in the fast-paced, often confusing world in which we live. Our romantic ideals lead us to believe that we can give unconditional and constant love and receive the same in return. When our husbands or wives tell us that they want a change—either in their own lives or in the relationship—we often view it as an assault on our union.

I know from firsthand experience that one spouse's desire for change can throw the other into a panic. Several years ago my husband decided that he wanted to stop practicing law to become a law school professor. At first, whenever he talked about it, I changed the subject. The kind of career move that he was contemplating meant a significant cut in pay. Frankly I was concerned about the impact his job change would have on our life-style, as well as the additional financial burden that would fall on me. After much agonizing I realized that having a frustrated, miserable husband with a big paycheck was not the foundation on which a strong marriage is based. With my blessing (given grudgingly) Michael switched careers. Much to my surprise, the change has been good for both of us. He loves his work and is extremely content. I, in turn, have the benefit of living with a man who is fulfilled because he is pursuing his dream. We have rid our marriage of a major source of tension and as a result are happier as individuals and as a couple.

From this experience I learned that although we resist change—I certainly did—it can be the best thing that ever happens to us. But I also understand how the desire for change on the part of one or both spouses can tear marriages apart. What if I had told Michael that I didn't want him to become a teacher? Chances are, we wouldn't be married today. We would both have become so angry and resentful toward each other, that we probably would have split up a long time ago. Yet, as I also learned, it is often very difficult to accept the fact that the person you think you married is not that person at all.

We often enter marriage with preconceived notions about the roles that we and our spouses will play in the relationship. It never occurs to us that we both may be called upon to play many roles or that the roles may keep changing. What many of us learn—usually within the first few years—is that our expectations bear little resemblance to the reality of married life. Since our marriages do not conform to our fantasies, we think that there must be something wrong. About half of us think that there must be something very wrong and decide to seek a divorce.

When couples are asked why they got separated, they often resort to clichés such as "We drifted apart" or "I don't know, we just grew in different directions." But these limp observations are not the real reasons. We all know couples who continue to fight and bicker long after the divorce is finalized although they are each ensconced in new relationships. We may wonder why they can't forgive and forget and start anew. But I will tell you why. Very likely one or both of them feel that they have been betrayed. The person with whom they fell in love, with whom they exchanged vows of lifelong devotion, with whom they expected to live their lives, suddenly changed—or so they think.

The errant spouse has violated the unwritten marriage

contract—the terms of their relationship—that every couple, knowingly or unknowingly, follows. They are no longer willing to perform the role in which they were cast—and we, in turn, accuse them of changing the rules in midgame. The angry husband might say to his wife, "What do you mean you don't want to be a housewife anymore? I married a housewife." The hurt wife might say, "What do you mean you want to be a teacher instead of a lawyer. I married a lawyer!"

And of course, we're wrong. We didn't marry housewives, lawyers, teachers, doctors, stockbrokers, or Indian chiefs, and neither did our spouses. We married people who may at any time decide that they want something more out of life or who, like us, have changed.

Change can be traumatic. Many late bloomers have rockier marriages than people whose relationships undergo few transitions. In fact, more than half of the late bloomers interviewed in this book were either separated or divorced. While not necessarily a representative sample, this could suggest that people who make changes in their lives are at greater risk of divorce.

Another reason why late bloomers may have more turmoil in their personal lives is that people who are looking for more out of life may not be willing to settle for less in a relationship. Many of us seek fulfillment everywhere—in our work lives and in our personal lives. Psychologist Dr. Paul Pearsall feels this is a trend for the better. Historically marriage was a union of survival and convenience, where people were so preoccupied with putting food on the table, that they didn't have time to think about much else. Today, thanks to advanced technology, we now have more leisure time to focus on our spiritual and emotional needs.

"We've moved from survival to thrival," says Dr. Pearsall. "We have more time to think about our relationships. A husband and wife now expect camaraderie, friendship, closeness, sexuality, the whole life spectrum."

Our higher expectations for ourselves and our relationships have altered our concept of marriage. In the "Me Decade," the 1970s, there was a cultural shift away from the couple to the individual. A controversial, best-selling book of that era, *Open Marriage*, by Nena and George O'Neill, proposed a new life-style for married couples. Suggesting that the traditional "we" approach to marriage was too stifling, the O'Neills advised us to focus on our own individual growth. Couples were urged to pursue their own interests as they maintained their separate identities. The most highly publicized aspect of the book was the authors' nonjudgmental approach to extramarital affairs. While they did not recommend sex outside marriage, they were "not saying that it should be avoided, either."

Five years and five million divorces later, in *The Marriage Premise*, Nena O'Neill wrote with great sadness about her own son's divorce. This book did not preach individuality but commitment, responsibility, and togetherness. I'm not suggesting that *Open Marriage* was responsible for the breakup of the family, merely that it was an accurate reflection of the mood of the 1970s. Similarly Nena O'Neill's second book revealed a growing concern over the skyrocketing divorce rate.

In a world where both partners in a marriage often work outside the home and pursue different interests, we maintain a greater measure of autonomy than ever before. If we pull too far apart, we run the risk of severing the ties that make us a couple. Maintaining a balance between our needs and the needs of our spouse is a major challenge of married life. What makes it all the more difficult is the fact that most of us came of age during a time when "we" marriages were the only marriages, where people stayed in unhappy marriages "for the sake of the children," and when men and women performed roles based on sexual stereotypes as opposed to personal preference. Our parents had fewer options and, therefore, fewer decisions. For those who conformed, life was much easier. For those who rebelled, life could be extremely lonely.

For instance, when my friend Linda got divorced in 1959, her mother urged her to tell people that she was a widow. "She told me that if I said I was divorced, it would ruin my chances of remarrying."

Given the mood of the times, her mother may have been right. In the 1950s there was a stigma attached to being unmarried or divorced. According to one public-opinion poll taken in 1957, 80 percent of the respondents agreed that for a woman to remain unmarried, she must be "sick," "neurotic," or "immoral."

By the 1970s the pendulum had swung violently in the other direction. Within twenty years the divorce rate had tripled. Divorce was no longer taboo. It was now being considered by many as a growth experience. The title of the best-seller *Creative Divorce: A New Opportunity for Personal Growth*, by Melvin Krantzler, said it all. We were no longer expected to make our marriages work, but to make the best of it when they inevitably failed.

It seemed that almost everyone was looking for something more outside the boundaries of marriage in real life and on the movie screen. *Kramer vs. Kramer* and *An Unmarried Woman*, two popular films of the era, dealt with different aspects of the divorce epidemic. In *Kramer* a harried, confused housewife abandoned an insensitive, workaholic husband and small son to find her own identity in a world where she had always been somebody's daughter, wife, or mother. In *An Unmarried Woman* a middle-aged man—presumably suffering from a midlife crisis—leaves his stunningly attractive wife to shack up with a sweet young thing he picked up at Bloomingdale's. Fantasy and reality collided for both rebellious spouses, who eventually regretted their actions. A guilt-ridden Mrs. Kramer fought for the custody of her son. An embarrassed husband whimpered that he wanted to come home.

On and off the movie screen there was a growing disillusionment with this new hedonism. Some of us who rushed into divorces found that it was not a panacea for all of life's ills. The emotional baggage we carried from one relationship to the next did not disappear with the divorce decree. Some of us who feared becoming a divorce statistic ourselves shied away from making a commitment. We drifted from relationship to relationship, practicing a form of defensive dating, breaking up with our lovers before they could break up with us.

Instead of moving closer together, men and women were stampeding farther apart. Critics looked for scapegoats. Back in the old days, when men were men and women knew their place, we didn't have these problems, they asserted. And in a way they were right. It was not just a coincidence that the growth of the women's movement corresponded to the astronomical rise in the divorce rate. When women throughout the country walked out of their kitchens and cried "We want something more," it created shock waves throughout the nation.

For one thing, a lot of men were left with a sink full of dirty dishes. I don't mean to be glib, but I really think that the backlash against the women's movement is not based on man's belief in his superiority over the "weaker sex" as much as it is on the inconvenience it has caused him on a personal level. In fact, in theory, most men support equal rights for women, as revealed in a recent Gallup Poll that reported that 64 percent of all men would vote for the ERA. As we will see, it's one thing to support feminism on a philosophical level and quite another thing to have to live with it. Take the case of John Rogers, a history professor and father of three, whose wife Sara quit her job teaching after they got married. All through their married life the couple focused on his career. In fact, every few years the family was uprooted so John could teach at a better university or take advantage of special fellowships. When he was finally settled in a comfortable, tenured position, he magnanimously encouraged Sara to get her Ph.D. in sociology. Reluctantly she went back to school, afraid that she couldn't compete with the younger students. Much to her surprise, Sara not only held her own but was one of the best in her class. Thrilled by her accomplishments, she began spending more and more stime studying at the university library. During a particularly hectic week when Sara was writing two papers and preparing for finals—a time when John was off from school—she became annoyed that he still expected her to maintain the household and care for the children singlehandedly. When Sara demanded that John now share in the housework, he became bitter and resentful. "John told me that he had always carried out his end of the bargain in our marrige—that is, he was the breadwinner. And he expected me to carry out my end of the bargain, which was taking care of the family. It didn't matter that I had assumed an additional responsibility. His attitude made me furious. I thought about all those years that I had done everything without complaining, and I thought, 'What a jerk I've been.'" Sara said angrily.

John did pitch in—he baby-sat for the kids on the weekend—but very grudgingly. Rather than put up with his complaints, Sara decided not to ask for any more help. As soon as she finished her degree and landed a teaching job at a nearby college, she and the children moved out. "And now, John's really fending for himself," Sara reported with great satisfaction.

Sara and John, like so many of us, had difficulty coping with a change in their relationship. From John's point of view, Sara had violated the terms of their unwritten contract by expecting him to make up for the time that she could no longer devote to housework. From Sara's point of view, John was being rigid and unfair.

The lesson that we all can learn from Sara and John's story is that when one person changes in a marriage, it has a tremendous impact on the other. Sara wasn't just asking John to do a little baby-sitting or to cook dinner occasionally, she was demanding that they alter the balance of power in their relationship. In the same way, when a husband switches jobs, he is not just changing the location of his office, he could be altering the dynamics of his marriage. Everything from the couple's social life to their sex life could be turned upside down by one seemingly minor change.

We often make the mistake of forgetting how the changes we make in our lives affect the ones we love. This is not to suggest that we should avoid change because of the impact it will have on others. Suffering in silence is not the answer.

119

Sharing our feelings and our needs with our spouses through open discussion can alleviate much of the anxiety they may feel about our desire for growth. I have talked with many couples who have accommodated enormous changes in their lives. These couples all had one thing in common. When one partner wanted to make major changes in his or her career or life-style, the other partner was included in the decision-making process. In other words, they did not say, "I'm unhappy. I'm going to do something about it." Instead, they said to their spouses, "This is how I feel. How can we work this out?"

In the beginning, it may be difficult for some of us to accept the fact that our husbands or wives may need a change. Consider the plight of the husband who is suddenly told by his wife that her desire to get more out of life means that she is going back to school and, therefore, will do less around the house. First, he's confronted with the unpleasant prospect of having to do more of the dirty work. Second, if he's been a dutiful breadwinner, he's bound to feel bitter that his wife is not living up to her end of the marriage bargain. And third, whether or not he admits it, deep down inside he's going to wonder, "Why aren't I enough for her? Why does she need more?"

Even a positive change can have serious ramifications on a marriage. For example, psychologist Arlene Kagle recently treated a man who had suffered from low-level depression throughout his seven-year marriage. His understanding wife had been extremely supportive and nurturing about his problem. Following therapy and prescribed antidepressants the husband was suddenly "reborn."

"Now, he wants to find out what he's missed all these years, and it's got to be threatening to his wife because some of those things don't include her," notes Dr. Kagle.

When one spouse suddenly grows, there is always a danger that the other will feel that he or she has been left behind. Suddenly being confronted with a happier, more fulfilled spouse can be very threatening if we no longer feel that we are needed. It's crucial for all of us to remember that when we make major changes, a little love and reassurance at the right time can let our spouses know that they are still a very important part of our lives.

If we proceed in a sensitive, caring way, changing the terms of the relationship need not terminate the marriage. It can be an enhancing and enriching experience for both partners. Spouses can and do learn to accommodate major upheavals in their lives if it means making their partners happy. For instance, when Patricia Ferrari entered law school, she had four children under the age of seven and one more on the way. Her husband, Robert, an attorney, encouraged her to become a lawyer although it meant that he would have to assume a greater share of the household responsibilities. Why did he agree to do it? To Robert it was a matter of basic fairness. "Even before feminism became a big issue, it occurred to me that there should be equality between the sexes. A husband should do things around the house and participate in the child rearing. It was the right thing to do."

Robert believed that the occasional inconvenience was well worth the price of making Patricia happy. But he's also gained something in the process. Not only is his wife a more contented, fulfilled person, but her paycheck has enabled the family to afford luxuries such as a second home and private-school tuition for their five children.

A partner with a leading New York firm, Patricia, who handles many matrimonial cases, often hears tales of woe from women who are in the midst of getting a divorce. "People often break up because of rigid expectations," she observes. "One person changes and the other can't handle it. I've changed tremendously during our marriage. I'm not the same person my husband married. We've both grown, and we've been able to accommodate that."

We hear a lot about divorce and not enough about couples like Patricia and Robert who have loving, caring relationships that not only allow for but thrive on change. It may be true that almost half of all marriages end in divorce, but an equal number last for a lifetime, and an extended lifetime at that. In 1900 the average person died before he or she was fifty years old. There may not have been as many divorces as there are today, but then again marriages were much shorter. We can now look forward to living on the average more than seven decades. Those of us who marry in our twenties or thirties and who stay together will be spending forty or fifty years with the same person. Because we are living longer and the world is changing at a faster pace than ever before, many social observers hang a cloud of doom over the fate of marriage as we know it. In his 1970 book, *Future Shock*, Alvin Toffler noted that if a successful marriage is based on couples growing together— the "parallel development" theory of love espoused by many marriage counselors—then marriage was heading the way of the dinosaur. He wrote, "In a fast-moving society in which many things change, not once, but repeatedly, in which the husband moves up and down a variety of economic and social scales, in which the family is again and again torn loose from home and community, in which individuals move further and further from their parents, further from their religion of origin, and further from their traditional values, it is almost miraculous if two people develop at anything like comparable rates." Just imagine what Toffler would have said had he factored in the women's movement, which was to transform the nation in the 1970s!

Yet, despite all odds, many marriages do last. Couples do develop and grow together to form strong, enduring unions. While we all may require change—excitement and stimulation in our lives—there is also a strong need to love and be loved. We can through love and communication form long-term relationships in which we bloom in synchrony.

In chapter two we introduced Martin Boris, a comptroller of a thriving chain of pharmacies who gave it all up in his midforties to become a writer. Now meet Gloria Boris, his wife of thirty-two years, who suddenly had to adjust to a major change in her life. Today Gloria can look back on it and laugh. A decade ago, when she sensed that her husband was extremely unhappy, it was a very difficult time for them both.

Although Martin couldn't keep his unhappiness a secret, he was very reluctant to tell his wife that he wanted to quit his job to become a writer. It was, after all, a radical departure from their extremely traditional life-style. Money wasn't a problem. They could live nicely on their investments and savings for the rest of their lives. At issue were their values and expectations. In Gloria and Martin's world, a man left the house every morning to go to work unless there was something wrong with him. A man definitely did not leave his job to write books. Although Gloria, with Martin's blessing, had resumed her teaching career after her children were grown, she made sure that everyone knew that she was not working for the money. Rather, she was another bored housewife who now needed something to fill her empty nest.

Gloria had noticed that something was profoundly disturbing Martin but was afraid to discuss it with him. Deep down inside she felt she knew the secret that had turned her warm, loving husband into a troubled, uncommunicative stranger: Martin was seeing another woman. She had read about such things in *Passages* and the *Ladies' Home Journal*. Even happily married men in midlife were bound to wander. Taking his imaginary infidelity quite philosophically, Gloria strategized how she would fight to get him back.

During the long car ride out to Montauk, Long Island, for a weekend in the country, Martin began to tell Gloria that he was unhappy. Her heart sank. "Here it comes," she thought. Beating him to the punch line, she calmly asked if he was involved with another woman. She was flabbergasted by his answer.

"He told me that wasn't it at all. He was unhappy because he wanted to write books. Books, I thought! Another woman I could handle. What could I do about him wanting to write books?"

After her initial surprise at his confession, Gloria became frightened. How could the father of three college-age youngsters quit work to write books? "I panicked," she admitted. "He kept telling me that everything would stay the same, that I wasn't going to be deprived of anything. It didn't help. All I could think of is, 'My God, we're not going to be able to pay the tax bill in April.' I was angry. How could he be doing this to me?"

Despite Gloria's misgivings, Martin was insistent. Nothing could make him change his mind. Given no choice,

Gloria reconciled herself to his decision.

It was rough going at first. Gloria felt awkward leaving her husband home in the morning when she left for her teaching job in Brooklyn. Her mother, who would call her daily, didn't help matters either by demanding to know, "What do you mean Martin's working at home now? Does he have a new business?"

Within a short time, though, Gloria began to notice a change in Martin. The man who was once tense and preoccupied seemed much happier and content. She also admired the long hours he devoted to his writing, thoroughly enjoying the chapters he gave her to read.

Gloria and Martin's relationship was undergoing a transformation. Uncertain of his ability as a writer, Martin looked to Gloria for emotional support. He openly discussed his anxiety over whether or not his book would ever get published. A novice navigating an unknown course, Martin needed all the encouragement he could get. Deeply in love with her husband and fully aware of the importance of her role, Gloria met the challenge. "All of our married life, he was the strong one," Gloria observed. "Whenever anything bad happened, he would keep it from me because I would fly off the handle. I didn't want to hear about anything that wasn't good. Now, for the first time, he turned to me for help and I guess I liked it."

The Borises grew together, but each in his or her own different way. As Martin developed into a creative, accomplished writer, Gloria became more independent and self-assured. Change affected their marriage for the better.

As it would be for many of us, it was difficult for Gloria to revise her expectations of the role a husband is supposed to play. If we enter marriage, or any relationship for that matter, expecting someone to follow our script, we will be in for a shock when they begin improvising on their own.

More often than not, the kinds of changes that Gloria and Martin made are good for a marriage. If we want to stay married to the same person, we can't expect that person to stay the same. We must give each other room to grow within and outside the relationship.

When a couple blooms together, it gives each partner a chance to explore untapped talents and abilities. Sometimes a role reversal can be refreshing and invigorating for both of them. For instance, the husband who held down a nine-to-five job for several decades may now enjoy pursuing a home-based vocation. In turn, the wife who kept the home fires burning for all those years may be eager to do something outside the confines of her home.

A change in life-style brings out the best in both of them. Such a couple is Paul and Millie Savitt. In his midforties, Paul gave up a partnership in a highly successful New York advertising agency to become a full-time artist. He, his wife, and their three daughters moved from Manhattan's posh Upper East Side downtown to a combination artist studio and apartment loft in Soho. At that time, Soho, just south of Greenwich Village, was a new Bohemian community that had sprung up in an area of abandoned warehouses and factories.

While Paul was starting his new life, his wife, Mildred, was starting a new chapter in hers. An interior decorator by training, she began designing and marketing unique pieces of jewelry. The small business she began in 1977 has blossomed into a major jewelry company. The talent seems to run in the family. Their daughters, Janis and Michelle, are also highly acclaimed jewelry designers.

I was referred to Paul by a mutual friend who casually described his work as "quite good." But I was totally unprepared for what awaited me when I visited Paul's loft one early spring day. His work—big, colorful, and a joy to look at—reflects his love of the primitive. With his bare hands, Paul paints, pounds, and sculpts "every material under the sun" into his own primal creations. "I'm like someone out of one of those old movies where they uncover a caveman who's been preserved in the ground," he joked. "That's me."

But Paul also has a sophisticated, urbane side reflected in a highly successful advertising career that began at the young age of seventeen. Paul was born and raised in New York City, and his artistic talent surfaced early. While attending a public high school that specialized in industrial arts, he won a prestigious citywide student-art contest. After graduation, he worked as a free-lance illustrator for well-known magazines such as *Collier's* and *The Saturday Evening Post*. The money came pouring in. "I was the only kid on the block with a convertible," he boasted. At twenty-one he married Mildred, who gave birth to the first of their three daughters the following year.

Paul had mixed feelings about being a commercial illustrator early in his career. On the one hand, he not only enjoyed living well but felt obligated to make as much money as possible to support his family. On the other hand, he had always dreamed of being a serious artist. He resolved these conflicts by vowing that one day he would have enough money to leave the business world to paint full-time. Until then he would have to be content to rent a studio near his Midtown office, where he would often paint from dawn to the start of the workday.

While Paul pursued his career, Mildred was the model

wife and mother, keeping house and chauffeuring the girls to their various after-school activities. An intelligent, energetic woman, Mildred admits that she sometimes thought about doing something else but felt being available to her daughters was more important.

After growing by astronomic proportions, Paul's graphic design company was transformed into a full-service advertising agency. Despite his success, Paul wanted something more—he still wanted to be an artist. In his midforties, Paul reached a critical point where something inside him said it was now or never. "I think there's an inner clock in every man and woman that lets you know when it's the right time to get moving. I was getting to the point where I no longer wanted to be a double agent. I could no longer be an advertising man and a painter and still have the energy to do both well." Selling his share of the business to his partners, Paul made a clean break with the past.

At the same time that Paul was freeing himself of the outside commitments that hindered his progress as an artist, Mildred was starting to look outside her home for fulfillment. Her daughters no longer needed her in the same way they had when they were younger. Although they were close to their parents, they were extremely busy with their own activities. In fact, since their early teens, they had been running a small business in which they designed and sold jewelry to department and specialty stores.

One rainy weekend Mildred entertained herself by designing three pieces of jewelry. Curious to see what her creations would look like, she hired a craftsman to carve them out of ivory. She showed the finished pieces to a friend, who, impressed by Mildred's work, offered to try to sell them. Much to her amazement, Mildred's designs went quickly, bringing in several hundred dollars within a few days. From that point on, Mildred began designing and selling her own jewelry, expanding her collection to include pieces in gold and precious stones.

Within a short time, Mildred's business took off. Over the past decade, she and her daughters have made the Savitt name a formidable one in the jewelry industry. (In 1984 Janis and Michelle Savitt won the Coty Award.)

Paul's decision to become a full-time artist created surprisingly little upheaval for his family. He attributes this to the fact that his wife and daughters were so focused on their own lives that they were not preoccupied with his. "Which is how it should be," he said.

While Mildred is interested in her husband's career, she is not the kind of wife who lives through her husband's accomplishments. From 8:15 A.M. until 5:30 P.M. she devotes her full attention to her business. "What I do is very time-consuming. I don't even take a lunch hour because buyers can drop in at any time and I have to be there." This is not to say that they are not an extremely close couple. Paul drives Mildred to work every morning and picks her up at night. He is not being overprotective: He likes the opportunity to get out of the house to see people. They spend all their free time together, including weekends alone at their country home in the Hamptons.

The Savitts' lives are full of contrasts. From a hard-driving executive Paul became an artist who spends all of his time painting in his downtown loft. Mildred was transformed from a devoted homemaker to a successful jewelry designer and businesswoman, who spends most of her day in her uptown office. They both showed extraordinary flexibility in accepting each other in their new roles.

Noting that the change never put any pressure on their marriage, Mildred observed, "It makes a marriage more interesting if you change every now and then, whether it's where you live or what you do."

Paul, who is extremely proud of Mildred's success, believes that it is crucial for both members of a couple to maintain their individuality. "If someone wakes up every morning and he or she has a goal, something to do, something to accomplish that belongs to no one else, that has got to be a very healthy relationship."

It may appear as if the Savitts' story is a fairy tale in this era of divorce. But they are real-life people who can teach us all an invaluable lesson. From the Savitts we see how marriage can accommodate change—and even flourish—if both partners give each other room to grow as individuals and also devote equal time and energy to their relationship as a couple.

Blooming Apart

In an ideal world, all couples would grow and bloom in harmony. But sometimes, despite our best efforts, our marriages turn into a tug-of-war as we each yank in different directions. One day the rope snaps. Suddenly no longer part of a couple, we are forced to find our way in a new world. For most of us, divorce is one of the most painful and emotionally wrenching episodes of our lives. Few of us in the midst of ending a marriage can see anything positive about the experience. And yet many late bloomers, especially women, cited their divorces as the turning point in their lives that spurred them on to do things that they never before thought possible.

On their own—often for the first time in their lives—they are amazed to discover that they can survive, even thrive, without a man to take care of them. It is the Cinderella story in reverse. As soon as the Handsome Prince leaves the scene, these former wives and mothers begin to blossom.

I'm not suggesting that all divorced women are able to pick up the pieces of their lives overnight and embark on new and exciting careers. The growing numbers of single mothers on the welfare rolls reveal the desperate plight of many divorcées, who are confronted with the dual burden of both raising and supporting their children. Yet the women I interviewed—many of whom had stopped working after marriage—did achieve incredible success after their divorces. Several had gone back to school to get professional degrees. One turned a small family business into a multimillion-dollar company. Another became one of the most successful real estate brokers in New York City. Most of all they were happy. Happy with themselves, their children, and their ability to make it on their own. Interestingly enough, although many eventually remarried, often to men in similar fields, they did not stop working.

Other writers have expressed surprise at the contented lot of the divorcée. In *Pathfinders*, Gail Sheehy noted that "no small number of my highest well-being respondents had been divorced, although not usually recently." The authors of *Lifeprints*, a book based on a study of three hundred women, observed that "The self-confidence and zest for life of many divorced women came as a surprise to our interviewers. They set out expecting to find these women depressed and gloomy."

A number of factors contributed to the rise of these new Cinderellas. For one thing many of these women had perceived themselves as trapped in relationships where their growth was stunted. When they decided that they wanted something more, their husbands couldn't, or wouldn't, accept their need for change. Feeling stifled and frustrated, they ended their marriages so they could begin their lives anew. But it wasn't easy. They left or their husbands left them with mortgages to pay and children to feed. The economic necessity of having to support a family, often singlehandedly, made many mothers very inventive. Fate was also on their side. They got divorced at a time when opportunities were opening up for women and at a time in fact when society was ready for women stars.

A case in point is Nancy Merrill, a reporter for NBC–TV in Chicago. What's extraordinary about Nancy's story is that she became a well-known television personality—with no prior broadcasting experience—at age thirty-six, an unusual feat in a field that is dominated by youth.

It's hard not to notice Nancy when she enters a room, in person or on television. A strikingly attractive blond, Nancy typically wears bright, primary colors and unusual pieces of jewelry. Obviously she enjoys being in the center of attention, and yet she knows there's more to being a television reporter than just looking good. By her own admission, she is almost always working, either editing tape or studying background material to prepare for the next interview. She is especially proud of the time former President Jimmy Carter told her that she was the best interviewer he had ever encountered and of a more recent coup, an exclusive interview with First Lady Nancy Reagan who was moved to tears over the memory of her late stepfather and the trauma of the attempt on the President's life.

Twenty years ago, Nancy had no career goals whatsoever. A sophomore at Skidmore, she was swept off her feet by a brilliant Harvard student. It seemed a perfect match. After graduation they married, and Nancy taught junior high school while her husband completed an M.B.A. degree at Harvard. "That's what you did back then," Nancy recalled. "You got married, you taught school for two years, and you had a baby."

Right on schedule, they had one child quickly followed by another. Graduating at the top of his class, her husband landed a high-paying consulting job that took him away from home a great deal of the time. The responsibility of raising the children fell on her. Nevertheless, despite her loneliness, it appeared as if she had done quite well for herself. "Everyone thought it was a good marriage and I believed it too. The material things—country clubs, a Mercedes, and European trips masked the emotional emptiness."

By age thirty, Nancy began to sense that there was something wrong with her life, although she couldn't pinpoint the problem. She continued to go through the motions of being the good corporate wife, entertaining her husband's business associates and chatting with their wives about recipes and clothing while the men talked business.

When her husband came home at night and talked about his problems at work, Nancy surprised herself by the intelligent comments she contributed to the conversation. As she learned more about the business world, she reached a disturbing conclusion. "All my life I had been brought up to believe that men were smarter than women, that men were worthier than women. You shone only as much as you had a little bit of their light. I finally realized that I was as bright as any man. In fact, I was a lot brighter than most of the men I saw in important positions. It made me very, very angry."

For women such as Nancy who were raised to believe in "the male mystique" she described, there was no greater disappointment than when they discovered that men were just people. Some were smart, and some were dumb. Some were strong, and some were weak. As some women developed a more realistic view of men, their marriages were actually improved. But for others like Nancy, this new awareness often resulted in extreme anger.

While anger turned inward can have a paralyzing effect, it can be a powerful motivator if constructively channeled. In Nancy's case it provided the adrenaline she needed to free herself from a comfortable albeit unfulfilling life to venture into an unknown world. For the first time, she began to focus on her own aspirations.

Since she had always been interested in theater, Nancy enrolled in Emerson College to get a master's degree in communications. When her student project, a television medical series, was selected as the best out of her class of 150 by three network executives, Nancy decided to pursue a career in communications.

The energy she had once devoted to her home was now spent on establishing her fledgling career. Her job hunt was organized and methodical. Assuming that her age would prevent her from ever appearing in front of a camera, Nancy decided that she could parlay her writing and producing skills into a behind-the-scenes job. After spending several months researching and writing proposals for television programs, Nancy felt she was ready to offer her ideas to programming executives. The only problem was that she didn't know any. But that didn't stop her. She turned to friends and acquaintances for help. "I let everyone know that I was looking for a job in television, and I asked them if they knew anyone who could help me. I told them all I needed was an introduction and I wouldn't embarrass them."

Often she would be referred to people who worked at television stations, who, in turn, would introduce her to people in programming. Noting that people are often reluctant to ask for assistance, Nancy said, "All you're asking them for is a word or two to get you through the door, but you have to swallow your pride in order to do it."

Once she got through the door, Nancy made the most of her meetings. At every interview she would hand out an outline of her show proposals, as well as a thorough critique of the television station's lineup versus its competition's. Impressed by her enthusiastic presentation, many of the people she met gave her names of other people to contact. Although everyone was extremely encouraging, competition in the field was keen, and Nancy had not received any firm job offers.

As Nancy became more involved in her career, she separated from her husband. "I couldn't stay in that marriage," she explained. "My husband was brought up, as were all men of his time, to be the breadwinner, to be the center of attention in the home. In turn, their wives were supposed to play a secondary, supportive role that I no longer cared to play."

The job hunt continued. Although Nancy was getting tired of rejection, she kept up her momentum, meeting with any television executive who would talk with her. In an extraordinary stroke of luck, after an interview at the Boston ABC affiliate, the general manager noticed Nancy walking through the parking lot. Immediately spotting her on-camera potential, he asked her about her background. What followed were the makings of a modern-day fairy tale—well, almost. The station manager then arranged for Nancy to audition to co-host a new talk show. Although she was seriously considered for the job, it went to a more seasoned broadcast journalist. Rather than discouraging Nancy, the experience made her more determined than ever. A few weeks later, when she learned that a competing station, WBZ, was looking for a host for its new daytime talk show, Nancy badgered the station manager until he agreed to see her. "I told him that he couldn't afford not to hire me," she recalled, still a bit amazed at her aggressive approach. "I told him that I was the audience he was after. I had been a housewife, I had been through a divorce. I have kids. I understand the problems of other women." Much to her amazement he agreed.

So did the audience. Within a year "People Are Talking" became the top-rated talk show in New England.

After her divorce Nancy vowed that she would never remarry. Since she already had two daughters and was never lacking for dates, she saw no point in getting tied down again. She was also concerned that she would never find a man who would not be jealous of her other love—her career.

In October 1983, while serving as master of ceremonies for a charity function, Nancy met Robert Page, the president and publisher of the *Boston Herald*. Immediately attracted to this charming international news executive, she was delighted when he asked her for her phone number. Two dates later they had fallen in love. Their whirlwind romance was complicated when Robert was transferred to Chicago to become president and publisher of the *Sun Times*. After spending a few months commuting back and forth from Chicago on weekends, Nancy and Robert decided to get married. Nancy was committed enough to the relationship to uproot her children, as well as give up her hourlong program in Boston for "The Nancy Merrill Interview," a four-minute slot profiling famous people on the five o'clock news in Chicago. But unlike her first marriage, this one is compatible with her professional and personal aspirations. "We're both equals," she asserted. "At night over dinner, I talk about my work and Bob talks about his work. My success is his success and vice versa. We're very fortunate; our lives have blended together beautifully. I now have two stepsons and Bob has two stepdaughters. They're neat kids, and they all get along. Our life is a joy."

Noting that they're in similar fields, Nancy said it is a pleasure to share her experiences with someone who understands both the pressures and the joys associated with her profession.

While Nancy's success is extraordinary, her story is typical of women of her generation who, as she puts it, "fell out of love with the idea of love." Once Nancy realized that love alone was not enough to make her a complete person, she was free to develop her talent. After she achieved her career goals, she was free to fall in love again, but this time on different terms—as an equal partner.

Nancy is now in a marriage where there is room for both partners to grow, as individuals and as a couple. She is very lucky. Making a marriage work was never easy, but it is especially difficult today. In the past, when most couples adhered to traditional sex roles, there were fewer options and, therefore, fewer decisions to be made. Today, given our diversity of life-styles and the blurring of sex roles, we are all confronted with many more choices. And there are many more opportunities for change. All of these factors place a tremendous amount of pressure on relationships. Marriage is not only a romantic and economic union—it must also accommodate the needs and desires of two people. Some marriages crumble under the strain. Instead of growing up together, couples grow apart. But there are also many strong, enduring, and loving marriages in which both spouses work toward separate as well as common goals. What we can learn from couples like the Ferraris, the Savitts, and the Borises is that change can be incorporated into a marriage in a positive way. If we include our spouses in our dreams—and if we encourage them to pursue their dreams—our marriages will be constantly changing—for the better.

CHAPTER 6

Rebels and Searchers: The Lost Generation Finds Itself

Did you ever have to make up your mind?
And pick up on one and leave the other behind.
It's not often easy, it's not often kind.
Did you ever have to make up your mind?*

> *"Did You Ever Have to
> Make Up Your Mind?"*
> LOVIN' SPOONFUL

*T*he 1960's have long been associated with flower power, love beads, war protest, and the sexual revolution. But another, more basic, change was taking place in that era. Many young Americans entered a new time zone in which standard timetables no longer applied. It was as if an entire generation had called time-out. One example of how my generation bent time is the phrase "the sixties" itself. "The sixties"—or at least, the spirit of "the sixties"—actually extended well into the middle of the 1970s. So did the childhood of many of the people who came of age in the 1960s.

We became a generation of late bloomers, postponing the rites of passage long associated with growing up. We prolonged our education by dropping in and out of college and graduate school. We made it possible to have our cake and eat it too by delaying marriage without forgoing sex. We "experimented" with a variety of jobs rather than settling on one career. In short, we resisted making any decision that would lock us into a lifelong commitment.

Critics have labeled us immature and narcissistic because we insisted on marching to the ticking of our own time clocks. "This generation has had it too soft," they say, blaming our so-called character flaws on our "spoiled" and "permissive" upbringings. But that explanation is much too simplistic. It's true that we may have been spared the economic devastation of a depression or the upheaval of World War II. And it's also true that many of us grew up in a time of unprecedented prosperity that offered seemingly limitless opportunities. Nevertheless, we have had our own share of problems and disappointments with which we were forced to cope. I believe that in some respects, we may have had a more difficult time than past generations because we were denied the benefit of role models whom we could emulate. Even if we had wanted to, and many of us did not, we couldn't have followed in our parents' footsteps because the path they took bore little resemblance to the road that lay ahead for us. The world of our childhood no longer existed. In our late teens and early twenties, we were confronted with a new and confusing world in which we didn't know where—if any place—we belonged. For many of us, these changes were painful and a bit frightening.

Over the past twenty years, all of our lives have drastically changed, whether we admit it or not. For example, rapid growth in technology has dramatically altered the nature of work; many of the jobs listed in the classified section of newspapers today existed only in the minds of science fiction writers two decades ago. Our personal lives are also a radical departure from those of our parents. The women's movement and the sexual revolution not only blurred sex-role distinctions but permanently changed the relationships between men and women.

Changing economic conditions have also had a profound effect on our lives. Born during the post–World War II baby boom, most of us were raised in traditional families in which dad was the breadwinner and mom was the breadmaker. With a booming economy, mortgage rates at an unbelievable 5 percent, and a society that frowned on working mothers, few wives had jobs outside the home. The unprecedented prosperity that became a way of life while we were growing up can no longer be taken for granted. The economic roller coaster of the past decade has resulted in inflation, severe recessions, staggeringly high interest rates, chronic unemployment, and dangerously high government deficits. As a result, most women of our generation—whether we have children or not—must also bring home a paycheck to help make ends meet.

The economic and social upheavals of the past twenty years have created a generation that has abandoned traditional timetables as a means of survival. Many of us need to move slowly and cautiously, in order to find our own way through uncharted territory.

From Gray Flannel to Beads and Bells

> Little boxes on a hillside,
> Little boxes made of ticky tacky.
> Little boxes, little boxes,
> Little boxes all the same.*
>
> *"Little Boxes, Little Boxes"*
> MALVINA REYNOLDS

If there is one theme to the sixties generation, it is that our lives have always been filled with contradictions. We were raised in one world and forced to live in one that is completely different. Even when we were children, our parents created a world for us that bore little resemblance to their own. Our parents' world appeared to be one of conformity in which one life-style prevailed. At approximately twenty years old, women took their wedding vows to grooms who were on the average two-and-a-half years older than themselves. Shortly after a year, they gave birth to the first of their three children. Every day husbands in gray flannel suits commuted to work in the city, leaving their wives and children safely ensconced in suburbia.

You might think that such normal, predictable parents

would have raised children who were clones of themselves. But as we know, they didn't. They produced us, a generation of rebels and searchers, who, upon coming of age, challenged much of what our parents stood for. For us to understand why we reacted the way we did, we must first examine the atmosphere in which we grew up.

Between the baby-boom years of 1946 and 1964, there were seventy-seven million of us born, accounting for nearly one-third of all Americans alive today. During the peak boom years following World War II and into the 1950s, America was transformed into a child-centered country. With so many young, impressionable minds waiting to be molded, it's no wonder that a whole slew of enlightened professionals, such as Dr. Benjamin Spock, appeared on the scene to help mom do a better job. Children were no longer born, they were created. Child psychologists and pediatricians emphasized that children could not fulfill their potential unless they were properly loved and nurtured.

From the crib on, we were taught to "do our own thing." The rigid feeding schedules that were popular in the 1920s and 1930s were abandoned for the more flexible self-demand approach counseled by Dr. Spock. Some mothers were imbued with "Pygmalionesque" fantasies that if they tried hard enough they could create the perfect child. Gone were the days when children were seen and not heard; children became the center of the household. As one women's magazine noted, "a good suburb is one that puts the needs of its children first," and needless to add, a good family was one that put the needs of its children first.

For the sake of the children, couples moved to uniform, Levittown-style suburbs where the kids could run free in the backyards. For the sake of the children, couples stayed married, even if they were unhappy. For the sake of the children, women quit jobs to devote their energy to full-time motherhood. For the sake of the children, mothers became chauffeurs, shuttling their youngsters back and forth from various after-school lessons and activities.

Ironically, while conformity was a way of life for our parents, they were teaching us to express our individual needs and desires. While our parents scrimped, saved, and sacrificed, their children were denied very little. "The message was clear," explained public-opinion researcher Daniel Yankelovich. "Parents were telling their children that we're working so hard so that you'll have a better life. These parents were sublimating their own needs for self-expression for the sake of their children. In turn, the children were expected to live out the dreams of their parents."

But the world our parents dreamed about was hardly the world we encountered when we grew up. Instead it was a world plagued with violence, political assassination, the Vietnam war, and a nation torn apart by the civil rights movement. It seemed as if there was no rhyme or reason to what was happening. All we knew was that we were being propelled into a world that no longer made any sense. When we turned to our parents for help, many of us were shocked to see that they were more helpless in this new world than we were. As a result many of us felt displaced and lost. We knew that we didn't fit into the tranquil, conformist world of our parents, but we didn't know exactly where we did belong. We felt like trailblazers, searching for a place for ourselves in this chaotic environment. Our parents, who had sacrificed so that record numbers of us could go to college, were heartbroken when some of us did the unthinkable: We drifted off the college/career path they had so carefully charted to find our own roads to happiness. Raised with the belief that we had control over our lives, unlike our parents, we refused to conform to the world: We expected the world to conform to our needs.

When the world wouldn't conform to our specifications, we decided to change it. Disillusioned with our parents' way of life, we created the "counterculture," a reaction to what we saw as a materialistic, "bourgeois" society. We dismissed the values that our parents cherished—the work ethic, religion, family, patriotism, and the pursuit of the American Dream—as drab and middle class. While our parents had only one life-style from which to choose, we aspired to a society in which everyone followed his or her own life-style. As Charles Reich noted in his ground-breaking book on the counterculture, *The Greening of America*, we had started a revolution. "Their protest and rebellion, their culture, clothes, music, drugs, ways of thought and liberated life-style are not a passing fad or a form of dissent and refusal, nor are they in any sense irrational. The whole emerging pattern, from ideals to campus demonstrations, to beads and bell bottoms, to the Woodstock Festival, makes sense and is part of a consistent philosophy . . . and in time, it will include not only youth, but all people in America."

We may have liberated ourselves from the "oppressive" values of our parents, but in the process we created an enormous vacuum in our lives. We had rejected our past without having a clear vision of the future. Many of us spent our early adulthood searching for something that would give our lives meaning and a place to call our own. Many "boomer bloomers" have emerged from this confusing era with a successful integration of their youthful ideals and conflicting values.

After a decade of searching for a place for himself, baby boomer Herbert Ogden found his way back. For as long as Herbert can remember, he wanted to be a doctor—or at least, he wanted to be like the two doctors he had known and admired. Born in 1952 to a lower-middle-class family in upstate New York, Herbert looked up to his pediatrician, a small-town practitioner with a dynamic personality. "He was a bit of a father figure," Herbert recalled. "He was disciplined and hardworking and he expected a lot from me."

Later, as a high-school athlete who suffered from frequent knee injuries, Herbert's encounters with an orthopedic surgeon whom he deeply respected reinforced his desire to study medicine.

Herbert's father, a maintenance worker who rose to a management position at General Electric, was especially proud that his son would be the first family member to go to college.

"My whole family thought it was just wonderful. 'Herbie's going to college and he's going to be a doctor.' They had no idea what it was all about, what being a college student was like—especially in 1970."

Fourteen years later, in 1984, Herbert looks like a man straddling two decades. His hair is longer than the present-day fashion, wavy, with light brown curls. A mustache on his face, the sneakers on his feet, and the attire he is wearing in between—tweed jacket, neatly pressed trousers, and plaid tie—reflect his counterculture past.

In 1970, coming from a high school where students concentrated on sports, dating, drinking beer, and getting into fights, Herbert arrived at Hamilton College, a small but academically acclaimed school, expecting to find pretty much the same. He was completely overwhelmed by what he did find: a sophisticated student body deeply concerned about its very survival. As the Vietnam war was escalating, student draft deferrals had been eliminated. Campuses all over the country were being disrupted by student strikes and demonstrations.

College was a real culture shock. It was the first time Herbert had ever ventured out of the conservative community where he had been raised. Suddenly finding himself surrounded by people with strikingly different beliefs and life-styles, he didn't know how to respond to his new environment.

Following his childhood plan, Herbert was a premed major his first semester, earning respectable grades. By January, however, he had decided to drop science courses in favor of philosophy and comparative religion.

"It was the age of questioning," Herbert explained. "I couldn't think of any good reasons to be a physician, so I let it go. In all honesty, I didn't have the discipline to pursue it at that point. I was too busy discovering things about myself."

In his junior year, Herbert was profoundly affected by his parents' divorce. The close-knit family that he had turned to for stability had been shattered. Since his parents were so preoccupied with their own problems, for the first time Herbert felt an enormous responsibility for his own life. It was both a liberating and a frightening experience. While he was freed from parental expectations and possible disapproval, at the same time he was being set adrift in an adult world in which he wasn't sure he fit. Somehow he would have to find his own way.

Supporting himself during summer vacation as a construction worker, Herbert managed to get through college with average grades. "It was a miracle that I didn't drop out," he reflected. "Frankly I wasn't motivated enough to do anything else."

For many of Herbert's classmates, the revolution ended after graduation when, often under parental pressure, they accepted their place in adult society as up-and-coming stockbrokers, lawyers, doctors, and other respectable professionals. For Herbert, however, the adventure was just beginning. Forced to leave the predictable, secure academic environment, he had no idea what he wanted to do or where he wanted to go. Intrigued by a friend's description of a school out west that taught mountain climbing and wilderness-survival skills, Herbert packed his knapsack and hitchhiked to the National Outdoor Leadership School in Lander, Wyoming. After completing the rugged three-and-a-half-month training course, Herbert felt a greater sense of accomplishment than he did after finishing four years of college. "I found it thrilling," Herbert explained. "I wanted to climb everything. Climbing puts you at the edge of your control, your creativity, your composure. It pushes you to your limits."

Vowing to return to NOLS as soon as he could, Herbert went back to New York to a temporary job as a construction worker. A few months later, he received a call from a college friend, who had become general manager of a radio station in Maine, offering him a job of sales manager. Since it sounded more challenging than construction work, Herbert accepted the position. He threw himself into his job, discovering that his low-key selling technique was quite successful. A year-and-a-half later, when he became bored with business, he quit to fulfill a longtime fantasy to travel around the world.

Before setting out on what was to be a very long journey, Herbert visited his sister at a boarding school in New England. He promptly fell head over heels in love with her friend, Ruth. Herbert took a construction job in New York so he could see Ruth on weekends.

That summer Ruth and Herbert hitchiked out west to NOLS where he became an instructor. When Ruth went back to school, he visited a close friend in Buffalo, New York, where he impetuously signed a contract to teach at a school for dyslexic boys.

"I had no intention of doing this, but my friend had already committed himself, and I thought it sounded interesting. The school was looking for someone to teach physics, English, and general science. They didn't care about experience; they just wanted people who were bright, sensitive, and who could work with kids."

Herbert spent the year as a surrogate father, teacher, disciplinarian, and coach for a group of high-school-aged kids. The work was difficult and at times lonely. Yet he seemed to thrive in a position of responsibility.

That summer Herbert returned to NOLS as a mountain-climbing instructor. Keenly aware that the safety of his students was in his hands, Herbert studied physiology and emergency first-aid procedures. "The worst things that can happen in the wilderness are medical," he observed. "When you're out in the mountains, you're the doctor. If someone hurts himself or has a problem at a high altitude, sound judgment and immediate first aid are critical."

As he entered his late twenties, Herbert began to rethink

his approach to life. Most of his friends from college had settled down with families or careers. He had done neither. Unable to make a commitment to any job for more than a year at a time, Herbert still lacked any specific goals. While his relationship with Ruth had developed into a strong, loving one, there was no stability there either. Herbert was "the searcher," the curious, spontaneous kid who, at a moment's notice, would hitchhike thousands of miles across the country to drop in on a college reunion.

The nagging question that had sent him on his long journey in the first place had not been answered. Herbert still needed to know "Where in this big world do I belong?"

He answered the question with another question. "Just where do I *want* to belong?"

For the first time, Herbert began to think beyond the next day. At some point in the future he might decide to marry and have a family. Could he even consider getting married if he followed his present course? Would he ever be able to provide a wife and children with a stable home life? Herbert began to see that if he didn't make some conscious choices, the choices would be made for him by default.

After pondering his situation, Herbert realized that he knew the road to follow at age eighteen, but for a variety of reasons—some valid, some not—he had lost sight of his goal. Herbert still wanted to be a doctor. The realization saddened him because he believed it was too late to do anything about it.

One night, over a drink with an old college friend, Herbert confessed that his one regret in life was that he had not gone to medical school. His friend replied that there was still time to do it. Herbert felt it was impossible. After all, he was twenty-eight years old, and medical schools wanted

150

students fresh out of college. To make matters worse, his grades were far from impressive.

At his friend's suggestion, Herbert called the premed adviser at Hamilton to see if there was any hope. From the adviser, he learned that Bryn Mawr College had recently started a program for people with nonscience backgrounds who wanted to return to school to study medicine.

The program, a rigorous completion of the basic sciences, accepted only those students with proven intellectual and academic skills who had made a mature and responsible decision to become physicians. Herbert's past came back to haunt him. Not only did his college transcript show a D in biology, but his frequent job changes caused some members of the admissions committee to question his stability. The only thing working in his favor was his excellent college board scores that proved he had the aptitude, if not always the desire, to be a good student. In the final analysis, it was Herbert's determination that made the difference. In an interview with the dean of the program, he presented a strong case on his behalf, stressing that his desire to study medicine was much more than a whim: It was the logical evolution of his skills and interests. For the past five years, he had been practicing emergency first-aid in the wilderness. As a teacher of dyslexic children, he had developed compassion for the disabled. In addition, all his years of wandering had given him an insight into the problems of people. The dean was impressed by his background and experience, and Herbert was accepted into the program for the following fall.

In sharp contrast to his college career, Herbert got a near-perfect 3.93 grade-point average at Bryn Mawr. For the first time in his life he was motivated toward a real goal, with a clear vision of what he was working toward. The self-confidence and discipline he had developed at NOLS came into play. "Mountaineering made me aware of my abilities and how I functioned under pressure. A lot of students at Bryn Mawr are understandably nervous about making this change. They're concerned about how they're going to deal with the intensity of the program. I actually felt safe at Bryn Mawr. At least I didn't have to worry about an avalanche on the way to the science building."

In retrospect Herbert understands why he was unable to make a commitment to medicine at age eighteen only to return to it a decade later. Initially his desire to be a doctor was based on the desire to emulate a role model whom he respected. In contrast, his decision to pursue medicine in his late twenties was based on a greater understanding of what practicing medicine might entail. With that knowledge came the motivation to fulfill his goal.

In September 1984 Herbert Ogden's search ended when he became a first-year medical student at the University of Pennsylvania.

Herbert is typical of many in our generation in that it took him a long time to make a commitment in terms of either work or relationships. For many of us, making a commitment—making a decision that tied us into a long-range plan—seemed to be an oppressive chore.

As one baby boomer put it, "I didn't understand why people made commitments. I couldn't see what was in it for me. It seemed to be nothing but drudgery."

Why limit yourself to the monotony of monogamy when it was more exciting to change partners as often as you liked? Why settle on one major in college when it was more fun to switch every semester? Why select one career when it was more interesting to flit from job to job?

Commitment was seen as a way of limiting options to a generation that was obsessed with keeping its options open. In *The Greening of America*, Reich asserted that the nation's youth, by refusing to be tied down, was rejecting a society that was becoming highly specialized in terms of education and occupation. Reich pointed out that from elementary school on, students are forced to make ever-narrowing choices. By their late teens, they're expected to select a college major that will lead to a career. The result, noted Reich, "is a gradually built up picture of man as a creature who has one single 'right' vocation in life, the vocation for which he is 'best fitted' and for which he can be aptitude tested and trained. The choice is surrounded by great anxiety and doubt, particularly because the student may find that his own nature fails to conform to the expected norm."

Not making a choice, however, can be just as limiting as being forced into an early decision. Choices may be made for you by default. For example, a woman who postpones bearing children until her forties runs a much greater risk of infertility than a younger woman. Our career options may also be curtailed. Although age restrictions have been relaxed in many schools, it is still more difficult for older students to get into medical and other professional schools than younger ones.

Despite the risks, none of the baby boomers interviewed for this book said they wished that they had done things differently. Although it may have taken them longer to make a commitment, they cherished the years they spent as explorers, searching for the right path. When they finally found it, they excelled in their chosen occupations, almost as if they were making up for lost time.

It was especially difficult for baby-boom women to find

their way through this period of social upheaval. If men didn't want to emulate their father's rigid, work-oriented life-style, we were equally dismayed by the role models set by our mothers. In fact, many of the women I interviewed said that their mothers were not happy as homemakers and made no secret of it, and my mother was no exception. From an early age, I realized that she was bored a good deal of the time at home and would have been better off with a paying job. We grew up knowing what we didn't want, but we didn't see any alternative. With no one to show us the way, we were completely on our own.

Born in 1944, Vivian Shevitz was a bit too early for the official baby boom, yet her experiences typify those of the first wave of "new women" who had to find a place for themselves in a rapidly changing world. Vivian was raised in a typical, upper-middle-class home in Detroit. Her father, an attorney, was an influential community leader. Active in the Jewish Community Council, he was also the chairman of the Michigan Civil Rights Commission. Like most other women of her generation, her mother quit her job as a social worker after marriage to raise her family.

Though not particularly close to her father, Vivian was always somewhat in awe of his accomplishments. "He was a wonderful public speaker and he was a very well-respected man," she recalled. He died in 1971, two years after suffering from an incapacitating stroke.

Throughout her childhood Vivian had just assumed that she would grow up to be just like her mother—that one day she would marry, have three children, and be a housewife. In junior high school, she suddenly decided that she wanted to be a lawyer. "I really didn't think much about practicing law. I just knew that I admired my father's eloquence, and it seemed to me that he was in a much more powerful position than my mother. I think I realized then that my mother wasn't really happy staying at home."

A good student in high school, at her mother's urging Vivian applied to Smith, the prestigious Seven Sisters college. She was astonished when she was accepted. "It was quite an honor, so I went, although I hadn't given it very much thought," she said.

When her parents drove her from Detroit to the Smith campus in Northampton, Massachusetts, Vivian's mother confessed that her daughter was fulfilling her girlhood dream. Although her mother had always wanted to go away to a good college, her parents wouldn't allow her to leave home.

Vivian soon learned that life for her at Smith was hardly a dream come true. To Vivian it seemed more like a finishing school than a college. Surrounded by wealthy society girls who spent their weekends sunning in Jamaica, Vivian felt bored and out of place. It was 1962 and young ladies were still expected to be in the dormitory on weeknights at 10:30. Meals were served in a formal dining room where students chatted in hushed tones. Vivian remembers laughing at an elderly zoology professor who blushed at the word *reproduction*.

"I looked around me and thought, 'What am I doing here?'" Vivian said.

Smith girls were supposed to fraternize with their own kind—Amherst men. Vivian, however, quickly fell into the scruffy, guitar-playing "beatnik" crowd from the University of Massachusetts, which made her feel even more like an outcast at Smith.

Unhappy at Smith, Vivian committed what was an unthinkable act in the early 1960s: She dropped out of a top women's school and enrolled in the University of Michigan for spring semester. A change of scenery was not the answer. Ambivalent about her studies, Vivian took a semester's leave from school.

What happened to the intelligent, motivated high-school student who always got straight A's? "I wish I knew," Vivian said with a sigh. "I just found it all very disillusioning."

While taking a few courses each semester, Vivian worked part-time at a popular record store in Ann Arbor. Her zeal for studying had long since passed. Typically she showed up for the first day of classes to pick up the course materials and returned the last day to take the final.

At Smith, Vivian felt as if she were an anomaly. But back in Michigan, there were growing numbers of students who like Vivian, were starting to question the traditional values that had guided their parents.

While Vivian shared many of their beliefs, she wasn't ready to "drop out" of society either. She was caught between two worlds. On the one hand, she listened as campus radicals contemptuously accused establishment lawyers of being "pigs," and on the other, deep down inside, she wasn't sure that she agreed. "It was a very, very confusing time," she said.

Vivian managed to get through college with mediocre grades, in part to appease her parents who by this time were simply "beside themselves" at her behavior. "They didn't know how this could have happened to a nice Jewish girl from Detroit, and to be honest, I didn't either," she recalled.

After college Vivian stayed on at the record store, a hangout for local musicians. Intrigued by the world of rock music, Vivian learned how to play the electric bass and joined a band that performed at clubs in Ann Arbor and

Detroit. For a while, she seriously considered pursuing a career as a musician. But by her midtwenties, when several members of the group decided to go to California to "make it" in the music business, Vivian stayed behind. "I was getting older, and I was tired of the whole scene. There was no stability to it. It was too much of an abandonment of the values that I did have," she explained.

At twenty-six Vivian's life was turned upside down when her father suffered a severe stroke. Visiting him in the intensive-care unit, Vivian was shocked by what she saw: The vital, strong father she had always revered was now gray and weak, attached to all kinds of tubes and life-sustaining equipment. "It was the most startling moment of my life," she said. "From that point on I began to see things in a different way."

Overcome by feelings of guilt, Vivian felt that somehow she had let her father down. She also realized that he wasn't going to be around forever to offer financial and emotional support. Since she had chosen not to marry at a young age, she had better start figuring out how she was going to take care of herself.

Vivian knew that she needed a career that would offer economic stability as well as a more normal life-style. She thought about her childhood dream of becoming a lawyer but quickly dismissed it as impossible because of her age and poor grades in college. Believing that she couldn't have what she really wanted, Vivian searched for something that was within her grasp. When she was accepted into a master's program in remedial reading at Michigan, Vivian decided to become a teacher. Motivated to succeed, she got excellent grades and landed a job teaching first grade during a time when teaching positions were scarce.

But teaching in a stringent, bureaucratic school system was not the answer. Vivian resented not being allowed to design her own curriculum and being forced to follow a standard plan. In addition, while she liked children, she did not enjoy being a mother to twenty-five six-year-olds. "I hated to do things like 'Now let's all take our red construction paper and cut a big valentine,'" she said.

At thirty years old, Vivian longed for a profession that was both worthwhile and could offer financial security. She decided that regardless of the obstacles, of which there were many, she would try to become a lawyer because that was the one thing she really wanted. Her poor performance in college severely limited the schools that would even consider her application. She needed to find a school that would give greater weight to her future potential than to her undistinguished past. A friend of her family suggested that she apply to Brooklyn Law School, his daughter's alma mater. Vivian did better than that. She came to New York to speak to the dean on her own behalf. After the interview, she was told that she would be notified within three weeks if she had been accepted.

Vivian returned to Ann Arbor and literally took to her bed waiting to hear from Brooklyn. The only school that had accepted her so far was a small one in Los Angeles, a place where she had no desire to live. As she saw it, Brooklyn was her last chance to fulfill her dream. Three long, nerve-wracking days later, she received a letter offering her a position in the class.

Vivian never expected to do well in law school. Just getting her law degree would have been enough. For the first time, though, she found school interesting and challenging. Much to her surprise, she ranked fourth in her class after the first semester, and by the following year, she was the top student. After being honored as the graduating class valedictorian, she was selected for a prestigious judicial clerkship and then became a federal prosecutor. Today she is a partner in a small firm specializing in litigation.

Has Vivian found her place in the world? Yes and no. While she is no longer a rebel, Vivian has not entirely bought into the establishment either. "Here am I, virtually an establishment attorney, but I'm still betwixt and between," she mused. Pointing to her blue sweater-dress and boots, she added, "I don't wear three-piece suits to work unless I'm going to court. My outlook really hasn't changed that much. I'm still not sure where I belong."

Vivian's observation reflects the predicament of so many baby boomers who are still uncertain of where we belong— or, more precisely, where we want to belong. Like Vivian and, to an extent, Herbert Ogden, we are living in two worlds—the world of our parents and the world we are creating for ourselves. What many of us have learned is that there is no such thing as a perfect world. In order to grow and ultimately bloom, we have to make many compromises and trade-offs. If we still feel that we are "betwixt and between," it is because the world we are creating is, like us, a blend of old and new values.

Both Vivian and Herbert had to choose a life-style before they could choose how they were going to earn their livings. The need for a more stable, secure environment motivated them to reexamine their lives and, ultimately, put them back in touch with their early dreams. Although they both chose fairly traditional professions, Vivian is a lawyer and Herbert is going to be a doctor, their outlook on life has not changed that much since their "rebel" days. As Vivian noted, she still resists dressing the part of a lawyer, and as Herbert recently confessed, he is planning on finding the time after medical school to climb Mt. Everest. While they may each have chosen a conventional path, true to the spirit of our generation, they insist on maintaining symbols of their individuality.

Not every rebel's story has a happy ending. Some of us were swept away by the tides of change, completely overwhelmed by this new world. A few did not survive. "I lost some close friends," confessed one thirty-eight-year-old architect. "Drugs, suicide. It was almost a winnowing process. The demands were heavy. To be out there on your own with the luxury of not having to do something was a terrible burden."

It's ironic that in a generation so preoccupied with finding itself, so many of its members got lost. For some the excess of freedom and overemphasis on self-discovery led to years of aimless wandering. Slogans such as, "If it feels good, do it," encouraged experimentation with mind-altering drugs, alcohol abuse, and sexual promiscuity. For those caught in the hedonistic, self-destructive side of the revolution, it was a long, difficult road back.

David Mitchell* was born in 1950 to upper-middle-class parents who divorced a year later. Raised in an affluent suburb with two live-in servants, David had everything money could buy. His mother provided him with tennis, swimming, and golf lessons, as well as the best private-school education. Academically David was outstanding. The top student in his elementary-school class, his family had big plans for him. There was no doubt that David would go to Harvard and then either to law or medical school. David saw little of his father, an alcoholic who had remarried three times since his divorce from David's mother. "We'd talk on the phone on birthdays and on Christmas, but that was it," said David.

Although his mother and extended family of aunts, uncles, and cousins were caring and concerned, there was a void in David's life that he felt could never be filled. "There was no father figure to say, hey, watch out for this guy and look out for that. I stepped on every emotional land mine and got blown to bits."

At thirteen David was sent to an exclusive prep school. For the first year he did exceptionally well, finishing tenth in his class. The following year, while hanging out with some older classmates one evening, he joined them in a drinking binge to prove that he was one of the guys. The next morning they were able to pull themselves together and go to class. David woke up feeling like he needed another drink. He began drinking heavily and soon he plummeted to the bottom of the class and was placed on probation. "I just crumbled," David admitted. "I decided not to work. It was more important to be accepted by my peers than to get into Harvard."

David's drinking began to take over his life. After a semester of cutting classes more often than he showed up, he was expelled and sent back home. He managed to complete his senior year at a private school in New York. Refusing to accept that her son had a serious problem, David's mother sent him out west to college, hoping that he would outgrow this nasty phase. The first week at school, David managed to get his picture on the front page of the student newspaper for wrecking a dorm with eight other students. Drunk for sixty-eight days in a row, David was told to leave at the end of the semester.

Desperate to find a place where David would fit in, his mother sent him to a progressive, experimental college down south. His class of thirty-five was filled with exceptionally bright, creative students. The only problem was that, like David, most of them were alienated from society in general and their parents in particular. At school David was introduced to the world of drugs. Every trendy drug found its way to the campus, and David tried them all. Letting his hair grow down to the middle of his back, David had joined the counterculture. Although he was apolitical, he shared his classmates' disdain for middle-class values. They vowed that they would never become businessmen, and yet they had no idea what they would do when they left school. "I was just a weakling and followed what other people did at the time," he said. "It was also tremendously fun. Drinking and drugs was a way to get laid, which was basically what everyone had on their minds. I attempted to learn a little, there was a lot of intellectual activity; however, it was still secondary to the hedonistic experience."

Having dropped out of school, David spent the next year drifting from one blue-collar job to another to support himself. The alcohol and drugs had taken a heavy toll: He developed chronic hepatitis. His doctor warned him that if he continued to drink, complications from the disease would kill him.

David was shocked into a painful realization. "I knew that I didn't want to die. I believed that I had some potential in the long haul. But the way I felt, I was as good as dead. So I decided to start living for a change," he explained.

Having leaned on alcohol for so many years, he found that not drinking was a huge adjustment. At parties David had to learn how to socialize without playing the part of the drunk. "Without a drink, I didn't know what to do with my hands, or for that matter, with my emotions," he admitted. Nevertheless, he managed to stay off alcohol as he began to focus on other aspects of his life.

David wanted to find something that would give his life meaning but he didn't know where to turn. So he dabbled. Interested in acting and film, he took courses at various colleges and enrolled in some theater workshops. Occasionally he landed a job directing a film for a small production company or acting in an off-Broadway play. The work was neither steady nor financially rewarding. "I was still dreadfully unhappy. These were five lost and wasted years," he recalled.

Eager to find steady work that he enjoyed, David applied for a job teaching filmmaking at the private school he had done well in as a boy. Although the headmaster wanted to hire him, the board of trustees decided that they could not afford another teacher. A few weeks later the headmaster made David another job offer. A student at the school was giving them a lot of trouble. Although he was bright, he was falling behind academically and was having difficulty adjusting. Could David tutor the boy and try to get him back on track? Genuinely fond of children and desperate enough to try anything, David accepted the assignment.

For three months David set the student on a rigorous study schedule, setting long-term and short-term goals. Little by little he helped the boy develop academic and social skills that built up his self-confidence. Eventually his student began doing well on tests and showed a marked improvement in his behavior.

As much as David helped the boy, he was helping himself even more. For the first time in his life, he was doing something worthwhile and emotionally rewarding. Not only that, but he was good at it: He knew from firsthand experience the hell these kids were going through. "There's no trick that they can pull that I haven't pulled; there's no negative sentiment that they can feel that I haven't already felt," he explained.

The school sent David more students. Extremely pleased with his work, they recommended him to other schools. Today he is a much sought after counselor who works for a number of private schools throughout New York. In addition, David is studying for a master's degree in education and plans eventually to pursue a career in psychotherapy for children.

His professional success has given him the time and the desire to focus on his personal life. David, who until recently had been unable to sustain a long-term romantic relationship, has now been living with a woman for more than a year. Being able finally to make a commitment to someone is a big step in his life and one he attributes to his improved self-image. "For the first time in thirty-five years, I've been able to say to a woman, 'I love you.' I feel good enough about myself and about her to make that kind of commitment. I feel that I have something that I can offer to someone else and that I in turn am deserving of someone else's love."

Although many of David's problems were exacerbated by drug and alcohol abuse, as well as an absent father, what happened to David is symbolic of what happened to many members of our generation. As David sees it, the problem was that we had too many choices and too little direction. "We were like kids in a candy store," he said. "We were told that we could do anything that we wanted. There was always the nagging feeling that if you made a choice, you'd miss out on something. It was so confusing. We didn't know where we belonged or what we wanted to do."

David, Vivian, Herbert, and all the other "rebels" and "searchers" of the sixties were looking for a place for themselves in a changing, fast-paced world. What we all learned is that you don't find your place by wandering aimlessly. The way to discover where you belong is first to decide where you want to belong. And that means making a commitment to something or to somebody.

As the sixties generation finally found out, making a commitment can be the most freeing act of all. Narrowing down choices is not necessarily limiting—it can actually be liberating—in that it frees us to focus our talents and energies on something that will give our lives meaning and purpose.

CHAPTER 7

The Phoenix Syndrome

Most of us would rather not talk about or even think about death in general and our own in particular. I'm no exception. I procrastinated for weeks before sitting down and writing this chapter about endings because I expected it to be depressing and painful. But I was wrong. For me it turned out to be one of the most exciting sections in this book because, as we will see, it is not about death — it is about life. As emotionally wrenching as it may be, the loss of someone whom we love — and ultimately the acceptance of our own death — can give us a new beginning. In fact, many late bloomers cite the death of someone they deeply cared about — a mother, a father, a husband, a wife, or a close friend—as the event that spurred them on to turn their lives around. Like the phoenix, the mythical bird that sets itself on fire and then rises anew from its ashes, late bloomers "bottom out," achieving a level of misery that forces them to start over again.

The acceptance of the inevitability of our own death serves as the "ultimate deadline," forcing us to focus on our goals and reorder our priorities with an urgency we never felt before. Taking stock of our lives and making midcourse adjustments have long been associated with the much touted "midlife crisis," which some psychologists believe occurs at around forty. Some of us, however, will experience this intense period of self-evaluation after the death of a close friend or a family member. For others it will occur after a life-threatening accident or illness.

Losing a parent is one of the most traumatic experiences in our lives. No matter how old we are, we always remain our parents' children. When we lose a mother or a father, we lose something profound that can never be replaced.

Even though we may love our parents and they may love us, many family situations are far from ideal. Relationships between parents and children are very complex. Some parents manage to provide a home environment in which we thrive and grow; others, consciously or unconsciously, place emotional roadblocks in our paths.

"The death of a parent can be like somebody suddenly taking down the stop sign," New York psychologist Dr. Arlene Kagle observed. She cites the example of a dominant underachieving father who, although he appears to be very strong on the outside, is actually quite fragile. Sensing his weakness, his children may be afraid to show him up by becoming too successful, and so they hold themselves back in terms of education and career advancement. When the father dies, they are finally freed of the burden of protecting him and can move ahead at their own pace.

A different set of complications arise if we are the children of extremely successful parents. In this case we may feel inadequate and in conflict with our parents' accomplishments. Consequently we may not even try, or we may try too hard. For example, Ken Stone,* the son of a self-made millionaire, vowed that he would make a million dollars before he was thirty, five years earlier than his father had made his first million. After Ken graduated from business school, he used a modest trust fund left to him by his grandfather to open three fast-food restaurants in a new chain. While the business did well for a new enterprise, Ken thought that it should be doing better. So he sold the restaurants and invested in a small medical supply company. Within two years, disappointed with the return on his investment, Ken was back in the fast-food business. When his thirtieth birthday came and went and he still wasn't a self-made millionaire, he was devastated. So he went into yet another business—he opened a home decorating store. That same year Ken's father died of an unexpected heart attack. Ken, who loved his father, was extremely depressed for several months after his death. But after that Ken underwent a seemingly miraculous transformation. He stopped switching businesses every other year, focusing all of his energy on building up the one he had. Within five years, he had made his million dollars many times over. Ken didn't consciously make a decision to change; rather, his father's death freed him from his own unrealistic expectations. No longer feeling pressured to prove himself to his father, Ken stopped looking for overnight success. When he finally concentrated on doing one thing well over a period of time, he was able to achieve his goal.

Living in the shadow of a famous or well-known parent poses its own unique problems. If we achieve success, we often wonder if we earned it ourselves or if it was due to our parent's reputation or connections. Take the case of actress Candice Bergen, who in the early years of her career would often receive scathing reviews with such unkind lines as, "Miss Bergen performs as though clubbed over the head." In an interview in *The New York Times*, Bergen noted that she made the greatest strides in her career after the death of her father, Edgar Bergen, the well-known ventriloquist, in 1978. "His death left a space for me," she said. "I was able much more to live according to my own expectations. I always felt my fame was ill-gotten, sort of borrowed from his, and that perhaps I tried to keep some kind of rein on it."

Since her father's death, Bergen received an Academy Award nomination for the film *Starting Over* and has written a best-selling autobiography.

New York therapist Judith White, M.S., C.S.W., director of public education for the Postgraduate Center for Mental Health in New York, notes that a parent's death often forces us to confront our own unhappiness. "We realize that we have a limited time to achieve our goals and life dreams. It can be very depressing and very overwhelming, but at the same time it can be an impetus to change."

Since so much of our adolescence and early adulthood is devoted to separating ourselves from our parents and establishing ourselves as individuals, we are bound to experience many conflicting feelings when a parent dies. If we allowed our parents to have undue influence on our careers or personal choices, we must now figure out for ourselves what it is we really want.

If we had a very dependent relationship on one or both of our parents, for the first time in our lives we will be truly on our own, as one late bloomer learned.

Janet Peters* admits that until her mother's death she was completely dominated by her parents. She not only relied on them financially, but she never made an important decision without consulting them first. Her father, a well-respected midwestern author, hoped that his daughter would follow in his footsteps. Janet, however, had neither the talent nor the inclination to write. In fact, she had very little interest in pursuing any career. Instead, when she graduated from college, she moved to San Francisco and took a secretarial job at an advertising agency. There she met and fell in love with Steve, an account executive. Although her parents thought that she could "do better for herself," they didn't try to stop her from getting married. Instead they tried to change their son-in-law into someone who conformed to their standards. Disappointed in Steve's choice of career, Janet's father continually badgered Steve to leave the "sleazy" business of advertising for a loftier profession such as law. They even offered to pay his law-school tuition. Instead of defending her husband, Janet would accuse him of putting her in an uncomfortable position with her parents. "I used to say, 'How could you do this to me?' But I wouldn't dream of telling my parents that it was none of their business. Looking back on it, I can see how unfair I was being," Janet said.

After the birth of her child, Janet quit her job to be a full-time homemaker. A second child soon followed. Thrilled to be grandparents, Janet's parents lavished expensive presents on her children, much to the annoyance of their father.

Once again Janet took her parents' side over his objections. Resigned to Janet's behavior, Steve stopped arguing. Instead he and Janet drifted farther apart, barely talking to each other except to discuss who would do what domestic chore and who would pick the children up from school.

When she was thirty-two, Janet was called back home to help her father care for her mother, who was dying of cancer. Janet soon realized that the father whom she had idolized was completely immobilized by his wife's illness. Incapable of doing even the simplest tasks, he relied on Janet to take care of *everything*. In addition to caring for her children, Janet spent six exhausting months at her mother's bedside assuming the roles of cook, nurse, housekeeper, patient advocate, and whatever other part needed to be played.

Janet remembers that her mother's last coherent words to her were, "Don't have a baby and then another baby and then suddenly find that you're fifty-three and dying. Please go back to work and do something with your life."

The words had a chilling effect on Janet. She was terrified that one day she too would be grieving over a wasted life. Yet despite her pain, something positive had happened over the past few months. Janet had finally grown up. "When my mother was sick, I was the caretaker. My father was no longer acting as a parent. We had switched roles permanently. I was nobody's child anymore."

A stronger, more mature Janet returned to San Francisco. Her homecoming was hardly ideal. Two days after her arrival, Steve told her that he wanted a divorce because he had fallen in love with another woman. "I really wasn't surprised," Janet admitted. "We didn't have much of a marriage. It had ended a long time ago, and I was hanging on because I didn't know what else to do. I wasn't angry at Steve. I realized that I was as much to blame as he was—maybe even more."

After their separation, Janet channeled all of her energy into finding a job. Janet called every business contact she had ever made and answered every help-wanted ad that struck her interest until she finally landed a management-training position at a major advertising agency. She is now a highly successful account executive.

The death of her mother was the turning point for Janet in that it forced her to confront her own mortality. It suddenly hit home that she had a limited time to accomplish her personal and professional goals. Throughout the ordeal of nursing her mother, Janet found that she had an inner strength that had previously remained untapped. Whereas before she was afraid to venture out on her own, she now felt confident to pursue a career and live her own life.

Just as overreliance on our parents can stunt our growth, having overdependent parents can be just as crippling.

When George Miller,* a Cleveland businessman, died in his early fifties, his widow Marlene was left with four children to raise on her own. She turned to her eldest son, George, Jr., age fifteen, for emotional support and assistance. George became the "man" of the family, assuming many of the responsibilities of the household that had previously fallen to his father, such as paying the monthly bills and disciplining his siblings.

After graduating from high school, George decided to go to a nearby college so that he could continue to live at home and help his mother. While his brother and two sisters moved out after or during college, George somehow couldn't bring himself to tell his mother that he wanted his own place. As Marlene got older, she grew more and more dependent on George. Although he dated a great deal, she never liked any of his girlfriends.

Suffering from severe arthritis in her late sixties, Marlene decided to live with her sister in the warm, dry climate of Arizona. She didn't expect George to leave his job to accompany her, but she made it clear that she wanted him to spend all his vacation time and holidays visiting her. George complied.

Finally on his own, George became engaged to a woman he met at work. They lived together on and off for five years. Within a year after George's mother died, they married and had a baby.

George acknowledges that caring for his mother may have prevented him from doing some of the things he wanted, but he has no regrets. "When Dad died, I did what I felt I had to do. Maybe my mother was wrong to place such a heavy burden on me at such a young age. I don't blame her; at the time she was helpless." Now happily married, George is quick to add that many of his college friends who married at younger ages are now divorced.

A parent's death may not only free us to do what we really want but also point up shortcomings in our lives. Take the case of the thirty-six-year-old man who had been raised by extremely frugal parents. Both victims of the Depression, they were obsessed with saving money "just in case." Their son, who had inherited their fiscally conservative practices, would forgo vacations and other luxuries although he could well afford them. He paid a personal price for his thrift. In his late twenties he had fallen in love with a woman who exasperated by his cheapness eventually left him.

When his father died, the son listened as his mother cried

and said, "We were planning on going to Europe one day," "We were saving to buy a place in Florida," and "We were just talking about visiting his sister in Los Angeles."

We were planning . . . we were saving . . . we were talking . . . It suddenly occurred to him that his parents had spent their lives postponing their dreams and now they had run out of time. Saddened by his parents' wasted lives, he re-evaluated his own life. Although he continued to be careful with his money, he stopped denying himself the things that he really wanted.

The death of a parent can also force us to confront the painful fact that there are some things in life that we cannot control. The twenties are a time when many of us feel invincible. At the peak of our physical prowess, we simply can't believe that there are problems that we can't solve or situations that we can't "fix." A case in point is the college drop-out who lost his father when he was twenty-four. An active participant of the "youth revolution" of the 1960s, he lived a reckless, day-to-day existence. "If it went fast, I did it; if it felt good, I tried it," he admitted. Needless to say, his father was disappointed with his son's freewheeling life-style.

After his father died, the son was distraught. Although he was sad that he didn't live up to his father's expectations, what really disturbed him was the shocking realization that death was final. Completely, utterly, and irrevocably final. No matter how much he wished, he couldn't make things right again. "I never knew anything that was irretrievable until my father's death," he said. "I was always able to screw up before and somehow I'd always land on my feet. I couldn't after he died. There was nothing I could do about it."

Sobered by his father's death, he began thinking about changing his life before he inadvertently did something to himself that was "irretrievable"—something that would inflict permanent damage on his body or mind. For a first step he stopped using drugs. Although it took him several years, he ultimately decided to finish college and go back home to run the family-owned car dealership. Today, as the happily married father of two, he is grateful that he was able to get himself back on track before it was too late.

Deadlines

In *Death Takes a Holiday*, a movie classic from the 1930s, the angel of death spends a weekend on earth to see what it's like to be human. While he's on vacation, the world is thrown into a panic. Without his help, people suffering from lingering illnesses simply can't die. Suicide attempts are thwarted. The old and tired, who are begging for eternal rest, can find no relief. The angel of death goes back to work, and all is well. The moral of the story is clear: Death is a necessary part of life.

If life went on forever, how would we plan our days? The timetables we live by today would be irrelevant. There would be no need for us to complete our education, start a career, or get married by any particular point in time because there would always be a tomorrow. With no end in sight, there would be no beginning.

None of us likes the idea of dying, of no longer existing as we know it. Yet the acceptance of the inevitability of death can be a tremendous motivator that gives meaning to life.

It's only natural to fear and even dread death. Despite what we are taught in Sunday school, few of us would be willing to trade our life on earth for the promise of spiritual eternity. For many of us, the thought of dying elicits a tremendous emotional response ranging from terror to rage. Working through the anger associated with our own death is a gradual process. Many of us do not confront these feelings until the death of a loved one forces us to contemplate our own mortality. In her ground-breaking book *On Death and Dying*, Dr. Elisabeth Kübler-Ross observes that we must work through our anger about dying before we can live life to its fullest. But as therapist Judith White observes, "Yet, for so much of our lives, we don't allow ourselves to get in touch with that anger."

The acceptance of death, of the finiteness of time, is very often the catalyst that helps us redefine our goals. It can also trigger very positive changes in our lives. As we reassess our dreams and ambitions, we may decide to alter our goals, to seek more obtainable goals, or to find new sources of fulfillment. For the first time, we may be able to focus on what is really important to us.

According to psychologist Daniel Levinson, coming to terms with death plays a major role in the adult developmental process. In midlife many men begin to question both the meaning of their own lives as well as the contribution they have made to the world. The denial of death is replaced by the acceptance of its inevitability and the desire for immortality. In his book *The Seasons of a Man's Life*, Levinson notes, "In the remaining years, he wants to do more, to be more, to give his life a meaning that will live after his death."

Most of us experience death secondhand in terms of

losing a friend or a relative. Few of us have had to deal with the possibility of our own death at a young age. Although it can be a terrifying experience, it can also bring about a heightened awareness that forces us to confront our needs and desires. The recognition that life is a precious gift that can be taken away at any moment is often the catalyst that provokes us into taking life-affirming action. After a near brush with death, Alice Byrne, a self-proclaimed housewife from the Mill Basin section of Brooklyn, made dramatic changes that altered the course of her life.

Alice, who is president of Ambassador Investigations, Inc., a private investigation agency, lives and works in a huge Victorian house in the residential section of Brooklyn where she was raised. The downstairs is devoted to offices; she, her husband, Tim, and two children from her first marriage—a teenage son and a daughter who is in college—live upstairs. An attractive strawberry blond with hazel eyes, Alice exudes warmth and a sense of humor. She appears to be amazingly calm and well organized. Although she has a staff of fifty-five, the half-dozen or so close associates who work with her say that she runs the business like a family. Alice is the first to admit that she was not raised to be the president of a big company. "Circumstances forced me into it," she admitted. "It was either that or welfare."

Throughout her childhood Alice fantasized about becoming an actress but never pursued it. When she graduated from high school, she asked herself the question that so many of us asked ourselves, "Now what?"—and like so many of us, she didn't have any answers. At her father's suggestion, she went to nursing school. After graduation, at twenty, she married a childhood friend whom she had been dating throughout school. Having recently lost both of her parents, she was overjoyed at the prospect of being part of a family again. The following year she gave birth to a daughter and five years later to a son.

Alice worked as a private-duty nurse at night so she could be home with her children during the day. In her free time she helped her husband establish a new business, a small security company that specialized in alarms. Although they were compatible business partners, their marriage started to deteriorate. "We were married very young, and we started growing in different directions," Alice explained. As church-going Catholics, the question of divorce never entered their minds.

But when Alice was twenty-seven, a shocking, unpredictable event turned her life upside down. The young, energetic, seemingly healthy woman had a heart attack. Refusing to be hospitalized because she and her husband had inadvertently let their health insurance lapse, Alice convinced her doctor she could administer the appropriate medication on her own.

Seeking a quiet environment away from her family, Alice went to stay at the home of Margaret, a longtime family friend who had always been like a second mother. During her convalescence she renewed a friendship with Margaret's son, Tim, who worked for an airline in Kansas City and often visited his family on weekends. Overcome by feelings of loneliness and isolation, Alice cherished the long talks she and Tim had on his weekend stays.

A few months later, Alice suffered another severe blow when she began to lose vision in her left eye. Her doctor, fearing she might have a brain tumor, prepared Alice for the possibility of surgery. Alice remembers this period as the low point of her life. For the first time, the normally cheerful, resilient young woman feared that she was actually going insane.

"It's hard to describe," Alice recalled, "but I was lying in bed and I suddenly felt as if I was in a spiral and I was going down. I was losing control. I don't know how to explain it, but I felt as if there was some lever I could pull to take control again. I don't know how I did it, but mentally I pulled the lever. I stopped the spiral."

The loss of sight was eventually traced to a blood clot that was dissolved through medication. Although Alice was beginning to gain back some of her strength, she was unable to return to nursing. Instead she worked at home helping her husband run the fledgling security business.

In 1973 an increase in international terrorism forced the Israeli government to look for a security company in the United States to guard El Al airlines. A business associate of Alice and her husband was offered the El Al business. Although he was reluctant to take on such a major assignment, the couple, eager for the experience, offered to manage the account. Within three weeks, they assembled a team of nineteen New York City policemen to moonlight as plainclothes guards.

As with any growing new business, survival was a day-to-day struggle. Although the couple continued to work well together, the marriage had not improved. At thirty-one, four years after her heart attack, Alice had a chilling realization. She no longer loved her husband. For a devout Catholic who came from a family in which no one had ever gotten a divorce, her feelings were both disturbing and confusing. Deeply aware of her own mortality since her illness, Alice knew that life wasn't going to last forever. Each day that wasn't lived to its fullest was a day lost. Alice agonized over her decision. "I didn't know what I was going to do," she said. "I didn't know the answers, I only knew the questions."

On a cold November evening before Thanksgiving in 1974, Alice told her husband that she wanted a separation. "I thought it would be temporary," she explained. "I still had not accepted the idea of divorce. All I knew was that I had affection for my husband, but I didn't love him the way a wife should love a husband."

Faced with two children to raise and limited financial resources, Alice continued working with her husband in the business. Eventually, they got divorced. When he remarried, they agreed it would be better if she bought him out. Borrowing several thousand dollars from a friend, Alice became the owner and president of Ambassador Security. She had five hundred dollars to her name, forty employees, and an abundance of anxiety.

"I didn't know what a debit or a credit meant. I couldn't type. I had never taken a business course. I had no management skills," Alice said, still a bit incredulous at her lack of experience. Her "survivor's instinct" and plain hard work guided her through the rocky days ahead. Aggressively seeking new business, Alice would stay up all night before meeting with a prospective client carefully researching and designing a comprehensive security plan tailored to the client's company. "I would go into each meeting thoroughly prepared," she explained. "Pretty soon word got around that we were good, and people started calling me."

After her divorce Alice's friendship with Tim blossomed into a romance. Although they wanted to get married, they decided to wait until Alice could obtain a religious annulment from the Catholic Church. It meant postponing their wedding for a year and a half, but to Alice it was well worth the wait. "I was trying to raise my children to be church-going Catholics, and it would have been hypocritical of us not to be married in the Church," she explained.

When the annulment was finalized, Tim and Alice set a wedding date for April 1978. Their happiness was shattered when a few weeks before the wedding Alice began seeing double and feeling weak. A battery of medical tests revealed that Alice had multiple sclerosis, a potentially debilitating illness. Since there was no guarantee that she would ever get well, Alice wanted to call off the marriage, but Tim wouldn't hear of it. "It could have happened a week after the wedding," he said. "What difference does it make?" On June 10 the couple took their wedding vows.

Alice didn't let her illness interfere with her life and made business calls from her bed when she felt too tired to work in the office. Within a year her eyesight improved as Alice began to feel well again. "I was getting stronger, physically, emotionally, and in the business."

Under Alice's stewardship the company became extremely successful, earning a national reputation for tackling difficult cases that other security firms had rejected. One of the most challenging assignments, a hunt for a missing California heiress, received a great deal of publicity. As a result Alice was invited to appear on a local talk show with another guest, Julie Patz, whose son, Etan, had vanished off the streets of New York City in 1979. After the program Julie asked Alice if she would develop a guide to help parents of missing children search for their youngsters. As a mother herself, Alice was deeply moved by Julie's plight. Alice not only volunteered her services to write the guide but helped organize the first National Missing Children's Day, a widely publicized event.

Despite Alice's impressive achievements, she was astonished when she was recently offered the presidency of Women Business Owners of New York, Inc., a support group for women entrepreneurs. "I couldn't believe that they were asking me, a housewife from Mill Basin, Brooklyn," Alice said. "I said to Tim, 'These are all businesswomen. I don't know why they want me. I'm out of my league.'"

But as Alice became active in the group, she began to realize that she was not only a businesswoman but a good one at that. "I've been in business for several years. I'm doing well. I have dozens of people working for me. I began to see that I have accomplished a great deal. I'm beginning to feel more confident about myself as a businesswoman," she explained.

The housewife from Mill Basin, Brooklyn, has come a long way. In spring 1984 she was on the front page of *The New York Times* presenting President Reagan with a tee shirt from Women Business Owners of New York, emblazoned with a slogan with which she can identify—"Women Mean Business."

Alice is not merely a success: she is a superachiever. Ironically if not for her heart attack or divorce in her late twenties, she might never have come close to fulfilling her potential. Faced with a business to run and a family to support, Alice rose to the challenge, transforming a small security company into a major private investigation agency. At an early age, Alice was forced to confront the possibility of her own death. Aware of the "ultimate deadline," she turned what could have been a tragedy into a positive experience that motivated her to become the person she was always capable of being.

New Beginnings

One day, after my husband and I had returned from the funeral of a close friend's father, I turned to Michael and said tearfully, "I never want to be left a widow." He thought about it for a second and then replied, "Well, then, I guess you'll have to die first."

I have to confess that I didn't like his solution any better, but his point was well taken. Death is inevitable. No matter how much we may hate the idea, one person out of every marriage will eventually be widowed. And usually it is the wife.

According to the 1981 census, there were 1,949,000 widowers as compared to 10,845,000 widows. Nearly one out of five women between ages fifty-five and sixty-four have lost their husbands. Since statistically women outlive men, the chance is four out of five that a wife will end up alone.

For the average married woman, this means at some point in her life she will have to start over again, all by herself. As strong and independent as we may be, contemplating the loss of our spouses is a terrifying and painful prospect. Our lives are so intertwined with those of our husbands or wives that when they die we lose a part of ourselves.

Losing a spouse is a devastating experience. The person that we are closest to in the world is suddenly gone. There are bound to be very painful and difficult times adjusting to no longer being part of a couple. Studies show, however, that life is far from over for the widowed. *The Inner American*, a study of American attitudes on a wide range of subjects, reports with surprise that widows and widowers hold a very positive view of themselves. The authors note, "This is an interesting finding. It may mean that people left on their own because of death of a spouse are confronted for the first time with the necessity of coping with life on their own." They add that the widowed "may discover new competence and gain self-esteem."

An example of this is Diana Wood, a nurse in her midtwenties whose husband, a physician, was killed by muggers in 1982. Pregnant at the time of his death, Wood had the baby on her own and is now planning on going to medical school. In an eloquent interview that appeared in *U.S. News and World Reports*, she said that although the pain "never really disappears," she was convinced that she was a stronger person than she was before the killing. "One of the worst things in the world happened to me, and I coped with it. I didn't commit suicide, have a nervous breakdown, or shut off my friends."

One life ends and we grieve and mourn our loss, and then like the phoenix, through our own efforts, we create a new life for ourselves.

A case in point is Florence Brooks. After a long illness, her husband, John Brooks, a prominent Southern California attorney, died, leaving Florence a widow at age sixty-five. Financially secure, Florence could have spent the rest of her life much the same way as before, filling her days with community work and her nights with the opera, the symphony, or playing bridge with friends. But since John's death, Florence had been experiencing feelings of boredom and restlessness that she had never felt before. The things she used to find challenging no longer held her interest. Florence was searching for something that would give her life meaning, but she had no idea when or where her quest would end.

Early one morning Florence was sipping coffee and watching "The Today Show," when an interview with the Director of the Peace Corps, Sam Brown, caught her attention. Citing President Jimmy Carter's mother Lillian as an example, Brown invited other older Americans to volunteer. Excited by the prospect of being needed and intrigued by the idea of traveling off to some distant land on her own, Florence called the phone number that appeared on the television screen to find out how to sign up.

The following week Florence received an application to join the Peace Corps. Attaching a three-and-a-half page letter listing her extensive community work—including the fact that she had singlehandedly organized twenty-six debutante balls—Florence returned the application, half expecting a rejection letter by return mail. Much to her amazement, two weeks later she received a telephone call from a recruiter in Los Angeles inviting her in for an interview. Both impressed by her desire to volunteer and amused by her background, the recruiter told Florence that somewhere, somehow, the Peace Corps would figure out a way to use her unique organizational skills.

To Florence, it sounded like a polite "Don't call us, we'll call you" rejection. Eleven months later she was stunned to receive a call from the recruiter who very excitedly told her that she had found a place for her in a country called Lesotho in the southern part of Africa. Would she accept the assignment? Without hesitation Florence replied "Yes!" and then sheepishly asked, "By the way, where is that?"

Although some of her friends thought she had lost her mind, her family was surprisingly supportive and understood her need to start a new life. After saying good-bye to her children and grandchildren, Florence packed the few personal belongings she was allowed to bring and began her long journey.

During training in Lesotho, Florence lived with forty-two other new volunteers in a cold, mountainous region where they studied Sesotho, the language of their new country. Having been away from the classroom for more than forty-five years, Florence was worried that she would not pass the language proficiency exam required by the Peace Corps. Despite her fears she received a top score and soon was sent off to the small village that would become her adopted home.

On a drab, rainy day, a truck deposited Florence and her two suitcases outside an eighteen-foot-wide mud hut with a thatched roof and two holes cut out for windows. She was greeted by a woman whose big smile revealed the one tooth left in her mouth. The woman was chattering away in rapid Sesotho. Florence blanked, not understanding a word that was being spoken. Eventually she was able to pick up a few phrases and followed the woman into the hut. As they sipped tea together and munched on lemon cookies, a great delicacy in that part of the world, Florence learned that her hostess was Masechaba Tebatso, the Chieftainess of the village.

"You are to be my daughter," she announced to Florence and gave her the native name Mamosa, which means "one who is good to others." In her halting Sesotho, Florence suggested that since they were more contemporaries in age, they should be sisters instead.

"No," insisted Masechaba. "If you were to be my sister, I couldn't tell you what to do. As my daughter, I will help you in your work, and every night I will personally put you into your bed. I will make you feel welcome."

For the next three days, Masechaba continually talked to Florence in Sesotho and like a dutiful mother tucked her in every night. On the third night, after she left Florence's hut, she stuck her head back in and said in perfect English, "Good night and sweet dreams." Florence raced to the door.

"You speak English," she exclaimed.

"Of course I speak English," Masechaba calmly replied. "My father was a Lutheran preacher who studied at a Lutheran mission eighty years ago. He sent me to the same mission where I learned English."

"How wonderful, we can speak English together, and I won't have to struggle with Sesotho," Florence said with relief.

Masechaba responded gently but firmly. "You are a guest in my country. As long as you are here, we will speak Sesotho. When I visit you in America, we will speak English." From that point on, Florence always addressed Masechaba in Sesotho, and a warm friendship grew between the two women.

Assigned to organize an experimental pilot program to teach the district inhabitants self-reliance skills, Florence worked side by side with the village chiefs. Her job required her to travel throughout the countryside to determine the most critical needs of the Basotho. Because of the scarcity of automobiles, Florence, who had never driven any car but a Cadillac back in California, got around the mountainous, unpaved terrain on a motorcycle. One day a nurse from the Peace Corps came to visit the village to check out some wild rumor she had heard about a sixty-seven-year-old volunteer who had been spotted on a motorcycle. Warning her that at her age a fall could result in serious injury, the nurse insisted that Florence trade in her bike for a truck.

Before arriving in Lesotho, Florence had been warned that living conditions would be primitive. It was difficult, however, for a woman coming from a five-bedroom, five-bathroom home to imagine just how primitive. Water was scarce. Florence was allotted sixty liters of water a week—a very little amount considering that it takes a full forty liters to flush a toilet. She had two small tubs of water in her hut. In the morning she'd rinse her face with the clean water in one tub and then put it aside in the other tub to wash her breakfast dishes. Later in the evening, she would rinse out her clothes in the same water, keeping it days at a time before throwing it out. Needless to say, the once-a-month bath in Maserv, the capital city some fifty kilometers away, was quite a luxury.

Florence is the first to admit that while she was able to teach the Basotho some of the ways of the western world, she also learned a great deal from the villagers she had grown to love and respect. A case in point was the time Florence started to cry because the garden she had so carefully planted and nurtured died as a result of lack of water. "Masechaba said to me, 'Stop crying, you can't change anything. If the good Lord wanted us to have water in this village, He would have given it to us. If He had wanted us to have good land, He would have given it to us. Since He didn't, and we can't help it, we're not going to cry about it.'" Florence said, adding with real admiration, "What a woman! What a philosophy!"

After twenty-seven months in Lesotho, Florence returned

home to California where she experienced severe culture shock. After the life of scarcity in Lesotho, she could not reconcile herself to the extreme affluence—and the extreme waste—prevalent in American society. "The amount of food that ends up in the garbage is obscene," she said indignantly. Instead of returning to her former life-style, Florence works as a recruiter for the Peace Corps in Seattle. One of her goals is to encourage other older Americans to become Peace Corps volunteers. A recent appearance by Florence on "The Today Show" elicited more than a thousand calls from prospective volunteers. "I'm effective," Florence said. "I'm outgoing and I like to talk about the Peace Corps. Also I'm seventy-two and people see me and think, 'If she can do it, I can do it.'"

Obviously not everyone is going to join the Peace Corps and ride around Africa on a motorcycle at sixty-seven or at thirty-seven. What makes Florence Brooks's story so relevant is not the exotic locale but the fact that she was able to start a new life at a point when many of us would feel that our lives were over.

At one time or another, we have all experienced an emotional blow that leaves us feeling as if our lives have ended. But as we can learn from people like Florence Brooks who have been there before, the hurt eventually heals. For some of us, it takes longer than for others, but we will emerge from the experience stronger and more resilient than before. With renewed energy and determination and a greater appreciation of life, we will blossom again.

CHAPTER 8

Helping Ourselves to Bloom

Finding Our True Calling

The men and women whom we met in *Late Bloomers* have done what we all want to do and what I believe is within our power to do. They bloomed. By that I mean they decided that they wanted something more out of life and committed themselves to achieving it. And so can we.

Blooming is not a passive process. If we sit around and wait for it to happen, it never will. We have to *make it* happen. But we can't expect to bloom overnight. It can take years, sometimes even decades, to fulfill our dreams. The way to make it happen is to systematically and methodically break down big dreams into smaller, more obtainable goals. Then we will succeed.

Almost all of us have taken the first step of the blooming process, the Realization, in which we have decided that we want more out of life. During the second stage, the Quest, we have to decide what it is we want. Some of us may know what it is we want, but for many reasons we're not doing it. During this period we will start asking ourselves why we strayed so far from our dreams and how we can get ourselves back on track. But there are those of us who have no idea what we want. We know we're unfulfilled, but we don't know what, if anything, will fill the void. We may have many conflicting interests that pull us in different directions, or we may not have found anything that interests us. Before we can bloom, we have to focus on a goal—a "true calling"—that excites and energizes us.

There are a great many misconceptions associated with finding our true calling. The term itself is misleading, because it suggests that for each of us there is only one "true" path to self-fulfillment. This is nonsense. For one thing some of us are multibloomers: we think that we have found our "true calling" in our twenties only to discover ten or fifteen years later that we are bored or dissatisfied and ready for a change. Our next career is no less of a "true calling" than our previous one. For another thing the entire notion of being "called" suggests that we have to wait for some kind of divine inspiration before taking any action. This kind of thinking makes those of us who haven't been called feel like there's something wrong with us.

We can take comfort in knowing that many of the most successful late bloomers in this book were not "called"— that they were forced to choose. Once they decided that they wanted more out of life, they actively sought out a goal that would infuse their lives with a special meaning and purpose. Consider the following examples:

—Martin Boris, a pharmacist, decided that he wanted more out of life. Feeling a strong need to be creative, he purchased an easel and a paint set and started painting. Within a few weeks, he realized that he had neither the talent nor the inclination to be an artist. Nevertheless, he had made a tremendous breakthrough. He had begun the process of self-discovery that would eventually reveal a talent in writing. Today Martin is a full-time writer and a published author. As we can learn from Martin's example, sometimes we don't know what our calling is until we try it. The Quest often requires *experimentation*—a willingness to try and fail and try again.

—Wally Amos, a struggling agent weary of the Hollywood rat race, decided that he wanted more out of life. He opened a chocolate-chip-cookie store for a very basic reason—baking cookies made him feel good. Today, Famous Amos Chocolate Chip Cookies are carried in stores all over the country. From Wally's story we can see that sometimes we have to *follow our instincts* before we can find our calling. Often our gut feelings lead us to the right path.

—Herbert Ogden, a mountain climber and self-described "adventurer," decided that he wanted more out of life. He was torn between his love for the outdoors and a strong interest in medicine. While he was debating which path to follow, he asked himself some tough questions. Where am I heading, and where do I want to be? Do I want a family and, if so, what kind of life do I want to provide for them? The more Herbert thought things over, the more he knew that in the long run he would be happier with the stable life of a doctor than with that of an adventurer who lived from day to day. Today Herbert is in medical school. During the Quest, we often undergo a *self-assessment period* in which we force ourselves to confront our true feelings. As we take stock of our lives, we review our likes, dislikes, beliefs, needs, and desires. As in Herbert's case, coming to terms with where we see ourselves in the future often helps us choose our present course.

—Betsey Nathan, a social worker, decided that she wanted more out of life. At her daughter's suggestion, she took the law-school entrance examination. She is now a third-year night student and a law review editor. Betsey is the first to admit that she would probably not have found her way to law school and an exciting new career without the help of her daughter. From Betsey's story we see that sometimes other people can provide the direction we are lacking. As we search for our calling, we must be *receptive to outside input*, seeking and accepting advice from people who may know us better than we know ourselves.

There are times when we may envy those people who know precisely what they want and who never stray off their life's path. But in a way they may be the ones who are missing out. The Quest to find our calling can be an exciting and rewarding experience that often has a surprise ending. We may discover new talents and skills we never before knew we possessed. Often we develop new ideas and interests that help round out our lives. And when we finally commit ourselves to fulfilling a dream, we move forward with a renewed sense of confidence and determination.

The Fulfillment

In the third stage of blooming, we identify—and over-come—the obstacles that have prevented us from fulfilling our dreams. Fulfillment is an ongoing process. Once we set our goals, each day we should move a little closer to achieving them.

Fulfilling our dreams—becoming the people we want to be—is also a complicated process. I wish I had a magic formula that could instantly turn our dreams into reality. But I don't. As we have learned from the stories of late bloomers, there is no one right way to bloom. We must all find our own way. But we can follow some of the examples set by late bloomers whose situations may be similar to our own.

Although the late bloomers in this book come from different social and economic backgrounds, they are strikingly similar in many ways. As a group they are extremely determined and persevering when it comes to achieving their goals. And in many cases, they have to be. For instance, when Herbert Ogden decided he wanted to go to medical school, he had several strikes against him. He was close to thirty years old (most medical schools prefer students fresh out of school), and he had poor grades in college and an erratic employment record. When Herbert applied to a special premed program at Bryn Mawr, the admissions committee questioned his stability. Refusing to be put off, Herbert met with the dean of the program and convinced her of his sincerity and ability. In turn, she convinced the committee to accept him. Had Herbert not vigorously fought for his acceptance in the program, chances are that he wouldn't be in medical school today.

Late Bloomers is filled with similar stories of people who pushed a little harder than others. They make the extra phone call, write the extra letter, and go on the extra interview. They believe in themselves, and more importantly, through their hard work they inspire belief in others. While it's true that persistent people are often the most successful whether they are late bloomers or not, I believe that late bloomers have an edge over others because they feel that they have to make up for lost time. They tackle their goals with a sense of urgency and energy that propels them forward.

Chicago television reporter Nancy Merrill is another case in point. At thirty-three, when she decided to pursue a career in television—a difficult field to break into at *any* age, but especially difficult for women past their midtwenties—she spent an entire year developing contacts. She asked everyone she knew if they could refer her to anyone who worked in television. Although she was interested in programming, she saw everyone who was willing to see her, whether they worked in the typing pool or the executive suite. They in turn would often refer her to someone who could help her. Eventually she landed a job hosting a daytime talk show.

Like other successful people, late bloomers have a knack for finding the right people when they need them. They reach out to friends, relatives, colleagues, business associates, and teachers. At critical points in their lives, they often find mentors. A close examination of this phenomenon reveals that it is not mere coincidence. For instance, when his career as a photographer was stagnating, on a trip to Atlanta Mark Rossi sought advice from a well-known local photographer. Prior to the meeting, the photographer had warned Mark that there were no job openings but offered to critique his work. Eager to make the contact, Mark made the appointment. By the end of the two-hour session, Mark had a job offer and a new mentor. Today he is a successful photographer. Had Mark not gone on the interview, his story might not have had such a happy ending.

The pattern is clear: Late bloomers do not leave the fulfillment of their dreams to chance. They decide to do something and find the means to do it. But sometimes we are unable to devote all our time to pursuing a goal. We may have other obligations or dreams that take precedence, or we may be reluctant to make a full-time commitment.

Depending on our dream, it may or may not be practical to pursue it on a full-time basis. Some late bloomers are financially secure enough to start over again in careers that may not pay off, at least in the short run. Paul Savitt, for instance, left a partnership in an advertising agency in his midforties to become an artist. But many of us are not in a position to walk away from a steady paycheck. This doesn't mean that once again we must abandon our dream. Not at all. Fulfilling a dream is too important to our emotional well-being to give it up so easily. What it does mean is that we must figure out a way to incorporate our dreams into our lives.

Some late bloomers overcame this problem by creating a transitional "rehearsal" period in which they eased into a new career while staying at their job. They did not suddenly quit their jobs and expect everything to work out for the best. Through careful planning and hard work, they prepared themselves to bloom, exploring their options without experiencing undue pressure. When they were ready, they made their move. Some of them, however, found that a limited involvement in a new and exciting endeavor provided the fulfillment that they were seeking. They became "dual career" people as they pursued two different dreams simultaneously.

Dual-careerist Jan Hobson is a late bloomer who juggles two completely unrelated jobs and loves them both. By day she's vice president in charge of advertising of Continental Bank of Chicago. After hours she is the owner of the Raccoon Club, where her singing group performs on Saturday nights.

Singing in rock and folk groups throughout high school, Jan abandoned her dream of becoming a professional singer in her freshman year at Northwestern University. At an audition for a school production, she was overwhelmed by the talent of the other students. "I started out with a lot of confidence in my ability as a performer," she said. "Northwestern was a very competitive school, especially in the performing arts. I was up against people like Shelley Long (of NBC's "Cheers"). After the audition, I lost my nerve." Refusing to try out for any more shows, Jan joined the school choir.

A communications major in college, after graduation Jan landed a job at an advertising agency. No longer with the choir, she stopped singing and concentrated on her work. By twenty-nine she was completely frustrated with her job, feeling that she wasn't moving ahead fast enough. Two friends, both copywriters, had recently collaborated on a book that was soon to be published. Jealous that they had managed to succeed in a creative enterprise, Jan yearned for a creative outlet of her own. A job change in the same field was not the answer. Jan wanted to get paid for doing something that she really loved, and the only thing that she really loved was singing.

Before her thirtieth birthday, Jan began taking singing lessons in preparation for launching her professional career.

A year later, she formed a vocal-harmony trio that specialized in songs from the 1920s and 1930s—"Jan Hobson and Her Bad Review" (sic).

Although singing gave Jan a great deal of joy, she was still discouraged at the office by her lack of progress. Fed up with her job at the agency, she went to work for a client, Continental Bank, as their advertising manager. Jan planned on keeping the job until she could support herself as a singer.

Jan's group began appearing in nightclubs throughout Chicago. Despite the hard work and late nights, Jan loved performing and promoting the group. Much to her surprise, she discovered that she was also enjoying her job at the bank. Receiving several promotions, she found the work to be quite interesting. In addition, her colleagues were more than supportive of her second career, vicariously enjoying her success as a singer.

As Jan and Her Bad Review became well known throughout Chicago, the group decided that they needed a new challenge. Jan toyed with the idea of bringing the group to New York to appear in clubs but ruled it out in favor of opening a nightclub in Chicago that would feature her group and other acts. For fifteen months, she searched for the perfect location. She found it in the River North, a former business district now beginning to attract art galleries, artist lofts, and night life. Late in 1984, the Raccoon Club, named after a song the group performs, made its debut.

Because her bank salary helps to finance her club, Jan is not planning on quitting her nine-to-five job in the near future. Money is not the only consideration. "I'm not sure that I would ever want to work only at the nightclub. I really do like having one foot firmly planted in the 'real world' of banking and the other in the artistic world," she explained.

Between the bank and the club, Jan often works eighteen-hour days. Despite the long hours, she is extremely happy. "To an observer, it may appear as if I am working ridiculously hard," she admitted. "I have a very rough schedule. It is a lot of work, a lot of detail, but it is also a lot of fun. I find it very rewarding, and there's nothing else that I'd rather be doing."

From Jan's story we can see that if a dream is important to us, we will find a way to incorporate it into our lives. While it may require careful thought and hard work, the satisfaction that we derive from our efforts makes it all worthwhile.

Late Bloomers is based on the stories of dozens of people like Jan, who after feeling dissatisfied or unfulfilled made a commitment to turn their lives around. There are countless numbers of other people who are potential bloomers: They feel that their lives are lacking and would like to do something about it. But because of fear, or inertia, or numerous other reasons, they remain frozen in their misery. The major difference between these frustrated, unhappy people and the late bloomers we've met in this book is the act of *doing*. Thinking about change won't make it happen. We have to make a decision to begin taking the steps that will lead to the fulfillment of our dreams.

For many of us the first step is the most painful. As long as a goal remains a private dream, we can safely indulge in our own fantasies where the outcome is assured. But as soon as we begin to turn our dreams into reality, we must confront the possibility of failure or disappointment. Some of us are thrown off course at the first setback. We assume that if we can't do something right the first time, it means that we can't do it at all. But as we've learned from *Late*

Bloomers, expecting too much from ourselves can be as damaging as expecting too little. For instance, when Helen Yglesias decided in her late teens that she wanted to be an author, she vowed to write only "great literary works." What followed was more than three decades of writer's block. In her early fifties Helen finally decided that she would be a writer because she felt a strong need to write, not because she wanted to be a great novelist. When she was fifty-four her first book was published. Ironically, by not even trying, Helen produced what many critics considered "a great literary work." This doesn't mean that we shouldn't strive to be as good as we can, only that we shouldn't cripple ourselves by setting impossibly high standards. And we should all expect to have our share of failures as well as successes.

Helen was held back by the fear that she wouldn't live up to her own expectations or the expectations of others. This is not uncommon. In fact, fear is the major reason why so many of us never fulfill our dreams. When we think of embarking on a new project or career, the excitement we may feel at the prospect of change is dampened by the terror of the unknown. If we let it control us, fear can paralyze its victim. If harnessed correctly, however, fear can actually work for us. The great English Romantic poet William Blake said fear is a "divine energy." In other words, fear can be a terrific motivator. A case in point is that of the landscape architect who had always believed that being "talented and fast on my feet was enough to get through life." When he graduated from college, he decided that he didn't need an advanced degree and started his own design firm. "I began to see that there were some very talented people out there who were also fast on their feet and who were also trained. They had gone to graduate school, they had the credentials.

I was scared. I knew I couldn't go up against them, not just professionally, but as a person, because I had never pushed myself to be as good as I could be," he said. Instead of giving in to his fear, he channeled it into making constructive changes. In his late twenties he went back to graduate school. He now has a Ph.D. in architecture and a thriving career.

Fear sometimes serves as a catalyst that helps us achieve our goals. Late bloomers often use the phrase, "I felt as if it was now or never," in describing why they changed the course of their lives at a particular time. In most cases the deadline was self-imposed. Realistically they could have postponed pursuing their goals until the next day, the next month, or the next year. Yet they felt a sense of urgency that made them believe they had to begin immediately. The fear of never starting—of never giving in to their true desires—literally scared them into action.

Setting a deadline—and sticking to it—can be an effective method of getting started. But there are some deadlines that stop us cold in our tracks. We decide that we are "too old" to do something and therefore we don't even try. For instance, I interviewed one woman who admitted that when she was in her late twenties, although she wanted to be a lawyer, she decided that she was "too old" to commit herself to three years of law school. A few years later she deeply regretted her decision. This time any reservations she might have had about her age were overridden by a strong desire to study law. She applied to several law schools and at thirty-one became a first-year student. She is now a partner in a small but successful law firm and is extremely happy. The lesson to be learned is that we are "too old" only when we believe we are "too old"—and when we want something badly enough, we don't let arbitrary age barriers or any other self-imposed roadblocks stand in our way.

The message of *Late Bloomers* is a simple one: There is no right or wrong time to pursue our dreams and goals. All of us develop and grow at our own pace, making changes in our lives when we feel that it's the right time for us. As long as we begin the process of becoming whoever or whatever we want to be, it doesn't matter if we are early, average, or late. Each of us will bloom in our own way, in our own time.

EPILOGUE

Late Bloomers *is based on interviews of* forty people—we know that there are countless numbers of you whom we were unable to talk to. Although not exclusively, the stories are primarily about achieving success in the world of work. We understand, however, that there are many other ways to blossom, and therefore, many different types of late bloomers. There are sexual late bloomers, slow starters in terms of personal relationships; there are spiritual late bloomers who are "born again" later in life. And, of course, there are numerous other stories of late bloomers in terms of business and professional success. In order to investigate this phenomenon further, we are asking any of you who are interested in sharing your story to write us about yourself. Specifically, we are interested in knowing why you think you are a late bloomer, what kind of change you made in your life, and what events triggered your decision to bloom. Your name and address is optional. Please let us know if you would be interested in being interviewed at some later date for a future book.

Please send your letters to:

LATE BLOOMERS/Carol Colman
Ballantine Books
201 East 50th Street
New York, N.Y. 10022

Carol Colman
Michael A. Perelman, Ph.D.

BIBLIOGRAPHY

Amos, Wally, with Leroy Robinson. *The Famous Amos Story: The Face That Launched a Thousand Chips*. Garden City, New York: Doubleday & Company, 1983.

Baruch, Grace, Rosalind Barnett, and Caryl Rivers. *Lifeprints: New Patterns of Love and Work for Today's Women*. New York and Scarborough, Ontario: New American Library, 1983.

Bloomfield, Harold H., M.D., with Leonard Felder, Ph.D. *Making Peace with Your Parents: The Key to Enriching Your Life and All Your Relationships*. New York: Ballantine Books, 1983.

Bolles, Richard Nelson. *What Color Is Your Parachute?* Berkeley: Ten Speed Press, 1984.

"Changes Are Noted in Marital Patterns." *The New York Times*, July 19, 1984.

Collins, Glenn. "First Portrait of the Very Old: Not So Frail." *The New York Times*, January 3, 1985.

Eck, Allan. "New occupational data improve replacement estimates." *Monthly Labor Review* 107 (3):3–10 (March 1984).

Gilligan, Carol. *In a Different Voice: Psychological Theory and Women's Development*. Cambridge, Massachusetts, and London: Harvard University Press, 1982.

Hagestad, Gunhild, and Robert Snow. "Young Adults Offspring As Interpersonal Resources in Middle Age." Paper presented at the annual meeting of the Gerontological Society, San Francisco, 1977.

Hall, Roberta M., and R. Bernice Sandler. "Academic Mentoring for Women Students and Faculty: A New Look at an Old Way to Get Ahead." Project on the Status and Education of Women, Association of American Colleges, 1983.

Henslin, James M., editor. *Marriage and Family in a Changing Society.* New York: The Free Press, 1980.

Hirshhorn, Larry. "Social Policy and the Life Cycle: A Developmental Prospective." *Social Service Review* 51 (3):434–50 (September 1977).

Jones, Landon Y. *Great Expectations: America and the Baby Boom Generation.* New York: Coward McCann & Geohegan, 1980.

Keniston, Kenneth. *The Uncommitted, Alienated Youth in American Society.* New York: Harcourt Brace & World, 1960.

Klemesrud, Judy. "Candice Bergen: Happy to Settle Down." *The New York Times*, April 13, 1984.

Krantzler, Mel. *Creative Divorce: A New Opportunity for Personal Growth.* New York: Signet, 1975.

Kübler-Ross, Elisabeth. *On Death and Dying.* New York: Macmillan Publishing Company, 1969.

Lasch, Christopher. *The Culture of Narcissism: American Life in an Age of Diminishing Expectations.* New York: W. W. Norton & Company, 1979.

Levinson, Daniel J. *The Seasons of a Man's Life.* New York: Ballantine Books, 1978.

Maslow, A. H. *The Farther Reaches of Human Nature.* New York: The Viking Press, 1971.

McBee, Susanna. "Here Come the Baby-Boomers." *U.S. News and World Report*, November 5, 1984.

—— "Are Today's Young a Disillusioned Generation?" *U.S. News and World Report*, January 23, 1984.

Naisbitt, John. *Megatrends: Ten New Directions Transforming Our Lives.* New York: Warner Books, 1982.

Neugarten, Bernice, editor. *Middle Age and Aging: A Reader in Social Psychology.* Chicago and London: University of Chicago Press, 1968.

Norton, Arthur J. "Family Life Cycle: 1980." *Journal of Marriage and the Family* 45 (2) (May 1983).

Bibliography

O'Neill, Nena and George. *Open Marriage: A New Life Style for Couples*. New York: M. Evans & Company, 1972.
—— *The Marriage Premise*. New York: M. Evans & Company, 1977.

Phillips-Jones, Linda. *Mentors and Protégés: How to Establish, Strengthen and Get the Most from a Mentor/Protégé Relationship*. New York: Arbor House, 1982.

"Public Opinion Referendum." *The Gallup Report* 229 (October 1984).

Reich, Charles. *The Greening of America*. New York: Random House, 1970.

Riesman, David. *Lonely Crowd: A Study of the Changing American Character*. New Haven, Connecticut, and London: Yale University Press, 1950.

Rubin, Lillian B. *Women of a Certain Age: The Midlife Search for Self*. New York: Harper & Row, 1979.

Sangiuliano, Iris, Ph.D. *In Her Time*. New York: William Morrow & Company, 1980.

Sanoff, Alvin P. "Baby-Boom Generation Runs into Reality." *U.S. News and World Report*, September 28, 1984.

Secunda, Victoria. *By Youth Possessed: The Denial of Age in America*. Indianapolis and New York: The Bobbs-Merrill Company, 1984.

Scheele, Adele, Ph.D. *Skills for Success*. New York: William Morrow & Company, 1979.

Schenkel, Susan, Ph.D. *Giving Away Success: Why Women Get Stuck and What to Do About It*. New York: McGraw-Hill, 1984.

Sheehy, Gail. *Pathfinders: Overcoming the Crises of Adult Life and Finding Your Own Path to Well Being*. New York: William Morrow & Company, 1981.

Slater, Philip. *The Pursuit of Loneliness: American Culture and the Breaking Point*. Boston: Beacon Press, 1970.

Terkel, Studs. *Working: People Talk About What They Do All Day and How They Feel About What They Do*. New York: Pantheon Books, 1972.

Toffler, Alvin. *Future Shock*. New York: Random House, 1970.
—— *The Adaptive Corporation*. New York: McGraw-Hill, 1985.

U.S. Department of Commerce, Bureau of the Census. *School*

Enrollment—Social and Economic Characteristics of Students: October, 1982 (Advance Report). Washington, D.C.: Government Printing Office, 1984.

Ventura, Stephanie J. "Trends in First Births to Older Mothers, 1970–79." *Monthly Vital Statistics Report* 31, supplement (2):1 (May 27, 1982).

Veroff, Joseph, Elizabeth Douvan, and Richard Kulka. *The Inner American: A Self Portrait from 1957 to 1976.* New York: Basic Books, 1981.

Walford, Roy L., M.D. *Maximum Life Span.* New York: Avon Books, 1983.

Whyte, William H., Jr. *The Organization Man.* New York: Simon & Schuster, 1956.

Wilson, Sloan. *The Man in the Gray Flannel Suit.* New York: Arbor House, 1955.

Wolfe, Tom. "The 'Me Decade' Decade and the Third Great American Awakening." *New York*, August 23, 1976.

Wood, Diana. "The Pain Never Really Disappears." *U.S. News and World Report*, November 14, 1983.

Yankelovich, Daniel. *New Rules: Searching for Self-Fulfillment in a World Turned Upside Down.* New York: Random House, 1981.

Yglesias, Helen. *Starting Early: Anew, Over and Late.* New York: Rawson, Wade Publishers, 1978.

INDEX

INDEX

About the Authors

Carol Colman, author of LOVE AND MONEY, is an award-winning reporter and the director of public affairs at WRFM radio in New York City.

Dr. Michael A. Perelman is a clinical assistant professor of psychiatry at Cornell University College of Medicine in New York City.